THE COMFORT *of* BOOKS & TEA

A Gentle Guide to Reading and Teatime

POE

THE COMFORT *of* BOOKS & TEA

A Gentle Guide to Reading and Teatime

FROM THE EDITORS OF *VICTORIA*

Hoffman Media
2323 2nd Avenue North
Birmingham, AL 35203
hoffmanmedia.com

ISBN 979-8-9923853-3-5
Printed in China

83 press

CONTENTS

INTRODUCTION

Author C. S. Lewis famously opined, "You can never get a cup of tea large enough or a book long enough to suit me," and we at *Victoria* heartily agree. Teatime adds gracious inspiration to our magazine, literary features lend storybook appeal, and often the complementary themes converge in a most beautiful way.

Within these pages, we celebrate the twin pleasures of reading and taking tea. Writers reflect on interludes of solitude in which one may sip a soothing blend or escape into a cherished volume, while editors explore the joy of sharing these pursuits with friends. Ideas for book clubs and other gatherings abound, as do recipes informed by childhood classics such as *Anne of Green Gables*, *Winnie-the-Pooh*, and the works of Beatrix Potter.

Flights of fancy take readers to Great Britain, a nation steeped in ardor for both the written word and refined refreshment. From a village brimming with booksellers and a tearoom tucked inside a library to sites associated with Jane Austen, these armchair journeys promise a multitude of bliss. Seasons unfold with tempting repasts and recommended reading lists. Finally, we peek into romantic abodes once inhabited by acclaimed novelists and poets. We hope these intervals of beauty stir the imagination and provide sweet reprieve for the spirit.

BLISSFUL PURSUITS

Few things are as restorative as basking in the serene companionship of a treasured novel and a fragrant cup of tea. With every turn of the page, the plot thickens, daily cares unwind, and gentle quietude descends upon the soul with each soothing sip.

BOOKS, DREAMS, FRIENDS

TEXT CAROL RIZZOLI

When a new year approaches, talk of parties, resolutions, and even housecleaning resounds, while inner thoughts turn, as always, to my oldest friends—books. Before siblings, before playmates, I possessed an entire world of friends on the shelf in my bedroom. The only permissible reason to get out of bed after being tucked in for the night with a book was to exchange it for another from a glinting row of Little Golden Books, each one savored and memorized. If hurried parents didn't recite every word, I knew and admonished them, according to my mother, "Don't turn page until you read all."

Everyone remembers, of course, the first books read on one's own, and among mine were the Nancy Drew mysteries. The lure of those particular stories, I see now, was the clever girl who took brave actions that many young girls then, certainly myself, never could have imagined.

Books, old-fashioned ink-on-paper books, still hold many advantages over their more modern iterations: first, the sight of a shelf full of color. At half a glance I see navy, umber, red, maroon, black, turquoise, gray, pink, green, white, and sky blue, along with myriad typefaces from the sleek and modern to those centuries old. Open a volume, and next comes fragrance: fresh, green, and inky if it's new, or a bit dusty and aged like a grandfather's cozy den. The scent hints at excitement, adventure, challenge, or comfort, dreams, memories.

Books provide a wonderful repository for souvenirs, too—a summer flower or lucky four-leaf clover pressed between pages and awaiting rediscovery, or perhaps a cherished inscription, even a forgotten letter. On a purely practical level, books work when there's a power outage.

Neither can you top the tangible social benefits of lending a book. One tells a friend or neighbor about a book, and then when the book is returned, further exchange ensues, and you may be lent a book you didn't even know about. Now that's social media!

And what about inscriptions? When you give a book and inscribe it to mark a milestone, there the inscription stays to be revisited and remembered. Especially touching, in my experience, are inscribed books that return to you once the recipient is gone. *Oh!* I thought, coming across a book I had given to my mother on one of her last birthdays. *I am so very glad I told her then what she meant to me.*

I bequeathed to my older daughter, Lucy, on her fortieth birthday a faded first edition of *Life Begins at Forty,* a gift from my husband that had cheered me through that milestone. Surprised and pleased, she had not heard of this book. A conversation followed about acquiring perspective on one's life, and in her voice I heard satisfaction at knowing what others, including her mother, had made of this turning point. Of course I inscribed it, and am guessing she will pass it on to her own children. Even better than one inscription is two or three!

"Open a volume, and next comes fragrance: fresh, green, and inky if it's new, or a bit dusty and aged like a grandfather's cozy den."

Book love, or book lust, runs in our family. One grandfather owned an antiquarian bookshop, which explains why I owned three glorious copies of the *Rubáiyát of Omar Khayyám*, each distinctively illustrated by a different artist. Then I came across my father's copy, so I kept it and gave the others to my three children. I still enjoy opening to the poem's most famous words: "... a loaf of bread beneath the bough, a flask of wine, a book of verse—and thou."

My own parents obviously loved books, and even our bookplates proclaimed, "There is no Frigate like a Book to bear us to Lands away." *Who said that?* I wondered, sitting down to write this essay. It was Emily Dickinson. Did my parents know that? I never heard her name until much later, at college.

Then my husband, Hugo, ran a bookstore that became a community gathering place: If you wanted to talk literature, art, travel, music, politics, or to exchange gossip—or just needed a good airplane read—this was the place. Families came, along with journalists, poets, politicians, and celebrities of varied stripes, and many a party celebrated an author's new book. It was also the place to go if you needed someone to walk your dog, as one of the obliging staff was sure to help you out.

And the holidays wouldn't have been the same at the bookstore without the annual visit of an elder statesman who arrived in pajamas, robe, and slippers to select gifts. Another customer, a gracious woman with her young son, attracted daughter Lucy's attention, and she volunteered to work for free on Saturdays, when they always shopped. "That's Wonder Woman," Lucy explained. "Don't you know?!"

But the single most meaningful book experience I remember came from an entirely unexpected direction. My younger daughter, Amanda, teaching that year at an elementary school across the country, phoned with discouraging news: The school library had been closed. Why? I asked, again needing the younger generation to provide explanation. Budget cutting, she said, in a school district with no clout.

Clearly, the only thing to do was gather up as many good books as possible and ship them to her. Everyone we knew had "too many books," and in no time, with help from our local school, I had seven hundred children's books packed in cartons. The unforgettable part came after the children opened the boxes, and each of Amanda's students got to take one home.

Reading their thank-you notes brought tears. "We never had a book at home before," one fourth-grader wrote. Another said, "The books are so cool, but I have a question for you. How can you guys buy all those books? Please write back soon." And this, partly in Spanish: "I felt sad when my dog died, but then I read a book about a dog, and I feel better." Most affecting of all? Maybe this: "How can we ever thank you? I wonder if our school can do something for you?" Just read, read, read, I wrote back.

So each year, as the calendar wanes, I stack up books as fortification for another New England winter, which gets going in earnest in January.

The books I'll peruse always include a few old favorites to be revisited and newer ones, including this year *The Hidden Life of Trees* and *The Inner Life of Animals*, both by Peter Wohlleben, both eminently enlightening and enjoyable. I'd read them quickly and want to know them better. Another in this category is *Gardens* by Robert Harrison, the single best book about gardens I know, as it delves into the surprising meanings of gardens through history and literature.

A third group is all the books I meant to read this year but didn't get to. I also plan to take down unknown books from our shelves, volumes inherited or subsumed into our collection from Hugo's bookstore, and get acquainted.

That's another advantage of books: The most patient of friends, they will wait for you as long as you wish. Some of these books have been waiting a generation or more for me.

Finally, upcoming selections of our neighborhood book club await, and I vow to get a head start on these. A feisty group that meets at all seasons in the oldest library building in the country, the Sturgis Library on Cape Cod, we gather beneath a portrait of an early town father whose stern gaze quells any thought of skipping a meeting or arriving unprepared.

By then it should be spring!

Brewing THE PERFECT CUP

A savvy hostess is keenly aware of the importance of serving teas that pair well with the various items on her menu. Offering a selection—perhaps a different choice with each course—allows guests to sample infusions that may be unfamiliar to them. It is always prudent to prepare and taste new varieties a few days in advance in order to refine steeping methods and to verify that the beverages will, indeed, complement the foods you plan to serve at your gathering. Here are some guidelines for making a perfect pot of tea:

❖ Start with good water.

If tap water is suitable for drinking, then it is suitable for making tea. If this is not the case, using bottled spring water is an alternative.

❖ Heat the water to the desired temperature in a teakettle on the stovetop or in an electric kettle.

Black teas and herbals can take boiling (212°) water; however, oolong, green, and white teas should never be steeped in water that hot, as it will impart an unpleasant, bitter taste to the infusion. Water between 170° and 195° is better suited for these delicate leaves, so be sure to consult the tea purveyor's brewing instructions.

- For black, heat to a rolling boil (212°).
- For green, heat to less than a boil (approximately 170°).
- For oolong, heat to less than a boil (190°–205°).
- For white, heat to much less than a boil (approximately 160°).

❖ If you plan to use a delicate vessel, warming the teapot first with a bit of hot tap water will avert possible cracking.

Pour this water out before adding the tea leaves and the water for tea.

❖ Use good-quality loose-leaf tea.

Loose-leaf tea usually yields the best infusions, and the leaves can be resteeped. This is especially true with oolongs, which often taste better on subsequent infusions.

❖ Add tea to the teapot.

Measure approximately 1 teaspoon of dry leaf per 8 ounces of water into an infuser basket or tea sachet set in the teapot. If you prefer a stronger infusion, add 1 or more teaspoons of dry leaf.

❖ When the water has reached the correct temperature, pour it over the tea leaves.

Place the lid on the pot, and steep. The brew time varies by type:

- For black, steep 3–5 minutes, or to taste.
- For green, steep 2–3 minutes, or to taste.
- For oolong, steep 1–3 minutes, or to taste.
- For white, steep 2–3 minutes, or to taste.

❖ Remove the infuser basket or tea sachet from the teapot to prevent oversteeping.

Note that oversteeping may result in a bitter brew. For optimum enjoyment, serve the beverage as soon as possible. Keep it warm beneath a pretty tea cozy or atop a lighted warmer.

BLISS DEFINED

TEXT OIVIA LUZIER

If you were to dig through my bookshelves and the many stacks of volumes piled in front of that library—as per Dr. Seuss's oft-repeated words: "Fill your house with stacks of books, in all the crannies and all the nooks"—you would find one of my most prized possessions: a more than 1,900-page, goldenrod-colored hardcover with speckled edges and gleaming gold lettering: *Funk & Wagnalls New Comprehensive International Dictionary of the English Language* (Encyclopedic Edition) from the year 1978.

Around fourth grade, I transformed from someone who hated reading into an absolutely voracious reader. I credit my evolution to wading slowly into the Harry Potter novels and consulting my grandma's eighties dictionary for so many words in the first two releases. Thanks to the combination of J. K. Rowling's series and that lexicon, once I saw and understood those terms, I didn't have to keep checking the dictionary. But I wanted to read it. With my expanding vocabulary, what else could I learn between the pages?

From then on, I devoured everything: annoying my best friend by reading nutrition facts aloud to her, poring over children's dictionaries cover-to-cover, swapping between fourteen not-for-school books at a time during breaks in class.

So, when my dad came home one day from a yard sale with this hulking gem of a tome from Funk & Wagnalls, I was thrilled.

I credit the reading of both fiction and my dictionary with how much my love for stories and language has grown. I've learned so much from this dictionary over the years by flipping through and lighting my finger on a word at random. Rereading it, saying it aloud, and then reading the next two pages of words and doing the same with those. Through this practice, I discovered words that sounded so intriguing that I used them later in my fiction writing as character names, creatures, or places. Entire ideas for some of my tales came from researching entries in this dictionary. Characters and plots blossomed as I held this resource across my lap and daydreamed.

But the story doesn't end there.

In my junior year of college, the campus library had a book sale to clear out old books no one was checking out. For two days, they opened up the back stacks for students to walk through the literal piles, in addition to ceiling-height shelves packed with books of every size, shape, color, and theme. Paperbacks for 50 cents. Hardbacks for just a dollar. Beautiful vintage finds for a dollar!

I was deep in the winding, labyrinthine stacks when I saw it: another dictionary bearing

a striking resemblance to the one that was the crowned jewel of my own bookshelf for years. I nearly dropped the stack of other dictionaries I was currently cradling in my arms. This edition was distinctly less ornamented, devoid of the goldenrod cover and the speckled-edge pages. Its cover was tan and bumpy, almost like a popcorn ceiling. Brassy matte-gold lettering introduced this neglected treasure as the *Webster's Third New International Dictionary* from 1971. It was starting to come apart at the bindings just a bit, but given some gentle handling, this thing would last. (And it has!)

Despite knowing that I was already leaving with an entire box of books that day (the librarians had given me one of the cartons that printer paper comes in), I couldn't leave without this dictionary. It needed to be with its peer! So, I ended up lugging about twenty-five books home, including the massive dictionary, in the middle of a snowstorm.

Yes, the day my wonderful boyfriend and I heaved a big box of books all the way across campus was in the drifts and slush of the worst snowstorm we'd seen during college. Many of those books later adorned the tables as centerpieces at our wedding.

I am, and will forever be, so in love with words. Dictionaries, and especially my prized pair, will always hold a special piece of my heart.

Earl Grey Rose Latte

Makes 2 to 4 servings

2½ cups **whole milk**
3 **Earl Grey tea bags**
¼ cup **granulated sugar**
1 tablespoon **rose water**
1 teaspoon **vanilla extract**
Garnish: **rose petals**

1. In a medium saucepan, heat milk over medium heat just until bubbles form around edges of pan (do not boil). Remove from heat and add tea bags. Cover and let steep for 20 minutes. Remove tea bags.

2. Return saucepan to medium heat. Cook for 5 minutes, whisking constantly, or until milk begins to steam again. Remove from heat. Add sugar, rose water, and vanilla extract. Pour into desired cups. Garnish with rose petals, if desired.

A quintessential British blend, Earl Grey is a black tea enhanced with the essence of bergamot. This small fruit boasts flavors reminiscent of orange and lemon as well as hints of grapefruit or lime. The perennially popular brew lends an intriguing complexity to a variety of recipes. While the citrusy notes of our highlighted blend shine in many desserts, it is the floral fragrance that advances in Earl Grey Rose Latte, gently pulled to the fore by rose water. A sprinkling of petals adds feminine charm to this simple yet satisfying beverage.

STAINED GLASS WORDS

TEXT CAROL BULLMAN

On bright mornings, when the stained glass window splashed a sparkling palette on the parlor floor, we sisters piled on the couch to peer through its red, blue, and green panes. Via that rectangular portal to the world, nothing appeared ordinary. It transformed our home, too, from an old Victorian in need of countless repairs to a beautiful work in progress. My father presented the window to Mama shortly after they bought the house, and she warned us to play very cautiously when we were near it.

I was brought up to think of books in much the same manner as that window. My parents revered them. Reading to us from the ends of our beds each night, my mother touched the book covers and pages with all the tenderness worthy of a newborn child. When Daddy pulled out a tattered, illustrated volume, we gathered round.

Anne of Green Gables; *Sarah, Plain and Tall*; *The Secret Garden*—Mama read them aloud to her four girls, and after we left that old house, she preserved them through all the moves. (Today, the tomes' beloved spines grace my bookshelf, ready to be plucked on a rainy morning or during a quiet evening, waiting for me to trace her invisible fingerprints back in time.)

My sisters and I eagerly anticipated trips to the library. Mama turned us loose in the maze of stacks, and we understood this: "Each of you may return with two jewels." The search for the perfect selections, the whispers among sisters, the stifled conversations with the gruff, white-haired librarian, the heavy clunk of the cards getting stamped—it was a marvelous ritual and one we couldn't wait to repeat every two weeks.

And, oh, the smell of those artifacts, marinated in the antique air of the tiny Greenville, Texas, library! Carefully opening a book, we smelled knowledge and fancy, coziness and elegance. We fell in love.

Although reading was often encouraged in our house and occurred almost daily, it never became mundane or was taken for granted. Books, for us, were not something to dive into with abandon, like a carton of movie-theatre popcorn. Instead, they were delights to be savored and protected. To this day, I have never read a book in a bathtub. I couldn't risk splashing those treasured pages.

Whenever my mother purchased a book just for me, inside the cover she penned a note and the date. My copy of *The Unicorn and Other Poems* reads, "As you researched and wrote your report on Anne Morrow Lindbergh, I think we both discovered a kindred spirit ... . I wish you many happy hours with this book. Love, Mama." At a used bookstore years later, what a find to stumble across a similar inscription from another mother—to hold in my hands layers of story upon story: the book itself, the love with which it was given, and the mystery of why it ended up in my possession!

My husband likes his Kindle, but I still prefer a candle flickering on an end table beside a cup of hot tea and me sitting with a friend whose cover I know—or will come to know—well, communing sacredly with another human being's highest thoughts. No Internet to intrude; no technological blips to stall the conversation.

The touch of my fingers on paper, the historical medium for the preservation of words, draws me closer to the text. Turning pages is a physical reminder of the privilege of reading—that within minutes I will be imbibing both words that flowed and sentences agonized over. I may read within hours what took years to write and lifetimes to learn or imagine.

Their multihued covers line my bookshelf. They are cherished gifts, like so many panes of stained glass, each offering a different glimpse of the world.

AMONG KINDRED SPIRITS

In the presence of dear friends, laughter and lively discussion flow more freely over steaming teapots filled with a favored brew and plates laden with delicious cuisine. Our fresh ideas abound for crafting menus and cozy milieus where stories can unfold beyond the page.

A Novel GATHERING

Settle before the hearth to discuss favorite volumes—enhancing time together by savoring a delectable menu that pays tribute to dishes mentioned in literature.

"For eating and reading are two pleasures that combine admirably," attests C. S. Lewis, whose The Lion, the Witch and the Wardrobe *inspires one of our recipes sure to enchant guests.*

Below left: Immersed in Heidi *by Johanna Spyri, many a reader has salivated at the description of Swiss cheese melting over a crackling fire. To satisfy this longing, our charcuterie board includes Appenzeller and Emmental, nestled among other morsels, including Roasted Potatoes. Above right: Reminiscent of Narnia, Turkish Delight tempts with notes of Chambord, rose water, and raspberry. Opposite: Mushroom and Onion Soup with Dutch Oven Bread brings to mind Sara Crewe's unexpected attic feast in* A Little Princess *by Frances Hodgson Burnett. The pairing also evokes a meal served in* The Remains of the Day *by Kazuo Ishiguro—a sign to aging English butler, Stevens, that the evening promises nothing "more daunting than an hour or so of pleasant conversation."*

Below right: A knave might have stolen the Queen's tarts in Alice's Adventures in Wonderland, *but our confections were purchased from a bakery. Present prepared treats atop a looking glass for a nod to the fantasy world created by Lewis Carroll. Opposite: An homage to Esther Bolick's signature dessert in Jan Karon's Mitford series, Mini Orange Marmalade Cakes feature ribbons of signature jelly between layers of fluffy cake crowned with creamy vanilla frosting and a sprinkling of fresh begonias.*

RECIPES

Roasted Potatoes

Makes 2 pounds

2 pounds **baby Yukon gold potatoes,** sliced in half
2 tablespoons **olive oil**
1 teaspoon **kosher salt**
1 teaspoon ground **black pepper**
8 to 10 sprigs fresh **thyme**

1. Preheat oven to 375°. Line a rimmed baking sheet with parchment paper.
2. In a large bowl, toss potatoes with olive oil, salt, and pepper.
3. Place on prepared pan with thyme and bake until golden brown, 30 to 35 minutes.

Dutch Oven Bread

Makes 1 (12-inch) loaf

3 cups **bread flour***
1 cup **white whole wheat flour***
1 tablespoon **kosher salt**
2¼ teaspoons **rapid-rise instant yeast**
1¾ cups plus 2 tablespoons **warm water,** (105° to 110°)

1. In a large bowl, place bread flour, white whole wheat flour, salt, and yeast; add 1¾ cups plus 2 tablespoons warm water, and mix by hand until mixture is fully incorporated and forms a sticky dough. (Alternately, place all dry ingredients in the bowl of a stand mixer, add water, and beat with the paddle attachment until a sticky dough forms, about 30 seconds.)
2. Cover and let rise in a warm, draft-free place (75°) for 2 hours. Refrigerate for at least 2 hours, preferably overnight, or up to 7 days.
3. Turn out dough onto a lightly floured surface. Lightly press dough just to level and even it out. Starting on the left side and working clockwise, fold edges of dough toward the center, pressing lightly, being careful not to create any air pockets.
4. Turn dough ball over, and using both hands, cup dough and pull it toward you (avoid re-flouring work surface, even if dough sticks slightly). Rotate dough 180° and repeat process 7 to 8 times, until you have a smooth, tight, sealed 10-inch oval. Applying even pressure, taper ends to yield a final length of 12 inches.
5. Lightly dust a piece of parchment paper with flour, and place the oval seam-side down. Lightly dust surface of dough with flour. Loosely cover with plastic wrap, and let rise in a warm, draft-free place (75°) for 1 hour.
6. When dough has 30 minutes left to rise, place Dutch oven and lid in the cold oven, adjusting racks to fit, if needed. Heat oven to 500°.
7. With a paring knife, score top of loaf.
8. Carefully remove Dutch oven from oven and remove lid. Using parchment as handles to lift loaf, carefully place loaf (still on parchment) in Dutch oven. Cover with lid and return to oven.
9. Immediately reduce oven temperature to 450°. Bake for 20 minutes. Remove lid; bake until an instant-read thermometer reads 200° when inserted into center of loaf, 11 to 13 minutes more. Immediately remove loaf from Dutch oven, and let cool completely on a wire rack before slicing or storing.

**We used King Arthur Unbleached Bread Flour and White Whole Wheat Flour.*

Mushroom and Onion Soup

Makes approximately 2 quarts

2 tablespoons **olive oil**
8 cups **Vidalia onions,** cut in half length wise and thinly sliced
½ teaspoon **kosher salt**
8 cups (¼-inch slices) fresh **cremini mushrooms**
2 tablespoons fresh **thyme,** roughly chopped
2 cloves **garlic,** minced
1 cup **dry sherry**
8 cups **beef broth**
Garnish: fresh **thyme,** fresh **white beech mushrooms**

In a large Dutch oven, heat olive oil, onions, and salt over medium heat, stirring to coat. Cook, stirring occasionally, until onions are caramelized, 35 to 45 minutes. Add cremini mushrooms, thyme, and garlic; continue to cook for 15 minutes. Add sherry and broth. Bring to a boil over medium-high heat; reduce heat to medium-low, and simmer for 40 minutes more. Ladle into bowls. Garnish with thyme and white beech mushrooms, if desired.

Turkish Delight

Makes approximately 80 pieces

1 cup **cornstarch**
4¼ cups **water,** divided
1 teaspoon **cream of tartar**
3½ cups **granulated sugar**
½ cup **light corn syrup**
1 tablespoon **Chambord**
2 teaspoons **rose water**
1 teaspoon **imitation raspberry extract**
1 drop **red food coloring**

½ cup **confectioners' sugar**, plus more for dusting

1. Line a 9x9-inch baking pan with plastic wrap and spritz lightly with cooking spray.
2. In a large enameled Dutch oven, whisk together cornstarch, 3 cups water, and cream of tartar.
3. In a medium saucepan, combine granulated sugar, corn syrup, and remaining 1¼ cups water, being careful not to get sugar on sides of pan. Bring mixture to a boil over medium-high heat, stirring occasionally to make sure sugar granules have dissolved, and cook for 8 to 9 minutes. Once mixture is boiling, do not stir. Cook, without stirring, until a candy thermometer inserted into center of mixture registers 230°, 7 to 8 minutes more.
4. Once sugar syrup reaches 230°, place cornstarch mixture over medium-high heat. Cook, stirring constantly, until mixture comes to a boil, 7 to 8 minutes. Let boil for 2 minutes, stirring constantly (mixture will be very thick). Turn off heat, leaving mixture on the burner.
5. Once sugar syrup reaches 250°, remove from heat. (Syrup can sit a few minutes off the heat if cornstarch mixture is not ready yet.) Carefully pour syrup into cornstarch mixture in batches, stirring well with a wooden spoon to combine after each addition. Bring to low boil over medium heat; reduce heat to medium-low and simmer, stirring frequently (every 5 to 10 minutes) with a spoon, scraping bottom and sides of pan, until mixture is thick and a light golden color, 1 hour 15 minutes to 1 hour 30 minutes.
6. To mixture, add Chambord, rose water, raspberry extract, and food coloring; stir to combine.
7. Pour mixture into prepared pan. Lightly spray a piece of plastic wrap with cooking spray, and place directly on surface of mixture, patting into an even layer. Allow mixture to set at room temperature for 8 hours or overnight.
8. Remove plastic wrap and turn out candy mixture onto a work surface lightly dusted with confectioners' sugar. Spray a kitchen knife with cooking spray and cut candy into 1-inch strips. Spray knife again and cut strips into 1-inch squares. Place candies in remaining ½ cup confectioner's sugar, rolling to coat. Store in an airtight container for up to 1 week.

Mini Orange Marmalade Cakes

Makes 8

1 cup **unsalted butter**, softened
2 cups **granulated sugar**
2 teaspoons packed **orange zest**
4 large **eggs, room temperature**
1 teaspoon **vanilla bean paste**
3 cups **all-purpose flour**
1½ teaspoons **baking powder**
¾ teaspoon **kosher salt**
¾ teaspoon ground **ginger**
½ teaspoon **baking soda**
1¼ cups **whole buttermilk**, room temperature
½ cup prepared **orange marmalade**
Creamy Vanilla Frosting (recipe follows)
Garnish: fresh organic **begonia flowers**

1. Preheat oven to 350°. Spray a 17½x12½-inch rimmed baking sheet with baking spray with flour; line bottom of pan with parchment paper.
2. In a large bowl, beat butter, sugar, and orange zest with a mixer at medium speed until fluffy, about 3 minutes, stopping occasionally to scrape down sides of bowl. Add eggs, one at a time, beating well after each addition. Beat in vanilla bean paste.
3. In a large bowl, whisk together flour, baking powder, salt, ginger, and baking soda. Add flour mixture to butter mixture, alternately with buttermilk, beginning and ending with flour mixture, beating until well combined.
4. Spoon batter onto prepared pan, smoothing top into an even layer. Vigorously tap pan on counter several times to evenly spread batter and get rid of as many air bubbles as possible.
5. Bake until a wooden pick inserted in the center comes out clean, 18 to 20 minutes minutes. Let cool completely in pan on a wire rack.
6. Freeze cake layer until firm, about 1 hour.
7. Invert frozen cake onto a large parchment-lined cutting board, and gently remove from pan. Remove and discard top parchment layer. Using a serrated knife, trim away uneven edges to create a 10-inch square in center of cake; reserve trimmings for another use.
8. Using a 2¼-inch round cutter, cut cake into 16 circles; place on a serving platter. Spread marmalade evenly over half of cake circles (approximately 1 tablespoon each); top with remaining cake circles.
9. Spoon Creamy Vanilla Frosting into a large pastry bag fitted with a medium open-star decorating tip*. Pipe frosting over tops of cakes. Garnish with begonias, if desired. Serve immediately.

We used a Wilton 1M decorating tip.

Creamy Vanilla Frosting

Makes approximately 1½ cups

½ cup **unsalted butter**, softened
⅛ teaspoon **kosher salt**
2 cups **confectioners' sugar** (approximately 8½ ounces)
2 tablespoons **whole buttermilk**
¾ teaspoon **vanilla bean paste**

In a large bowl, beat butter and salt with a mixer at medium speed until creamy, about 1 minute, stopping to scrape down sides of bowl. With mixer at low speed, gradually add confectioners' sugar to butter mixture, alternately with buttermilk, beginning and ending with confectioners' sugar, beating just until combined. Beat in vanilla bean paste until smooth. Increase speed to medium; beat until fluffy, about 2 minutes. Use immediately.

A BOOK CLUB PRIMER

Nothing warms the soul quite like curling up with a good book. Invite a coterie of fellow bibliophiles to a cozy gathering where you can chat about your latest reads while sipping a soothing cup of tea.

LINEBERRY.A.WILK

Book clubs can be rewarding, yielding meaningful friendships, stimulating conversation, and a well-informed oeuvre. But where to begin? There are many considerations and decisions to be made when establishing such a coterie, but let our guidance help you parse out the process.

Establishing the Preliminaries. On a spectrum from social hour to academic rigor, why do you want to start a book club? The answer to this question will help orient you to the tone and theme of your group. It can also help determine the level of discussion you expect from meetings and guide you when choosing members.

Putting a Face to the Name. Choose a moniker that suits your group and its mission—it can be clever or descriptive. The name can align with your club's identity, focus, or location. You may want to launch with a name, or recruit members first and then decide on one.

You might begin with a few friends and ask them to invite several people to meetings. Consider posting a notice on social media, either for online or face-to-face clubs; or the notice could appear at the library, bookstore, market, or other places you frequent that have community boards.

Especially if your club is oriented toward a certain genre, you may want to be selective when choosing members—readers of British literature only! Or perhaps you are seeking a more diverse group, with various viewpoints and literary tastes that will facilitate livelier discussions. Many seasoned book club leaders caution, however, to include those with like-minded reading styles to facilitate more rewarding discussions.

Another consideration is the number of members to include. Depending on the meeting location, consider how many people the space can comfortably accommodate. Some groups prefer to comprise five to fifteen members, others twenty or more. Keeping the group small ensures that everyone's voice will be heard and encourages the development of friendships among members.

Time After Time. Most book clubs tend to gather once a month, but those reading longer works may wish to meet every six weeks. Meetings can run as long as they need to, or you can set a designated start and end time, which may be necessary if your group meets for lunch or to otherwise allow for busy schedules.

During the winter holidays and summer, many groups go on hiatus to accommodate travel plans. It is a good idea to send meeting reminders through email or social media, depending on your group's preferences, two weeks prior and then a few days before the meeting.

Choices, Choices. Fiction or nonfiction? Poetry or drama? The vast body of available literature is rife with options. A club could read only the works of Shakespeare or perhaps be oriented toward works from the Romantic era. Choices could encompass all contemporary fiction, mysteries, or short story collections only. Or maybe your group will read widely across genres. Once you have chosen the thematic direction, you can determine new titles by following recommended lists, taking turns choosing, or voting on selections.

Location, Location, Location. Depending on the day and time your club meets, you can make use of public venues, such as the library, a clubhouse, church, or bookstore. Some cafés and restaurants offer discounts to groups that meet regularly at their place of business. Book clubs that take turns meeting at members' homes sometimes host a potluck, or the designated host can prepare a meal or snacks.

If your club will be meeting online, you may choose to take advantage of social media as a forum. You can create a private group on some social media outlets, where discussion (and visibility, if you choose) is limited to members only.

For many people, the advantages of online meetings are significant—there is no travel or need to designate a meeting space, no preparation (beyond the reading), and no cleanup. For others, though, meeting in person is a significant part of a book club. Whatever your preferences—online or in person—you are bound to find like-minded members.

For the Establishment. Usually, the person who starts the club serves as group leader, but some book clubs rotate leaders, or moderators, based on who chose the book or who is hosting a particular meeting. Leaders establish a precedent and serve as coordinators and disseminators of information, discussion questions, and meeting reminders; they are diplomatic initiators of good discussion and facilitators of group equity.

Leaders or another designated person (perhaps whomever suggested the book) will develop topics of conversation for the meetings. Some publishers include discussion questions or reading guides in books or post them online. Designate a chapter or chapters to read prior to the meeting. You can ask everyone to come prepared with at least one question to talk about.

Lifelong friendships can result from the bonds forged through book clubs, and at the very least, the time with your group should be joyful and filled with camaraderie. Regardless of your club's direction or philosophy, everyone should feel included and enjoy themselves, whether it is through socializing and light chatter or through headier, more intellectually stimulating discussion.

Our cozy setting celebrates the twin pleasures of reading and teatime with stacks of books and accoutrements of afternoon tea. Above left: For an artful accent, create posies in tea tins. Tuck a small vase in each canister, fill with water, and arrange stems for a brimful bouquet.

Earl Grey Lemon Cheesecake

Makes 1 (9-inch) cheesecake

¼ cup **heavy whipping cream**, room temperature
4 **Earl Grey tea bags**
2 cups **gingersnap crumbs**
¼ cup **unsalted butter**, melted
1½ cups plus 2½ tablespoons **granulated sugar**, divided
½ teaspoon **kosher salt**, divided
3 (8-ounce) packages **cream cheese**, cubed and softened
2 tablespoons **loose-leaf Earl Grey**, finely ground
3 tablespoons **all-purpose flour**
2 teaspoons **lemon zest**
3 large **eggs**, room temperature
¾ cup **sour cream**, room temperature
Garnish: **edible flowers**, fresh **blueberries**

1. In a medium saucepan, heat cream over medium heat just until bubbles form around edges of pan (do not boil). Remove from heat and add tea bags; cover and let steep for 20 minutes. Remove tea bags, squeezing to extract as much liquid as possible. Refrigerate until chilled, about 30 minutes.
2. Preheat oven to 350°. Spray bottom of a 9-inch springform pan with baking spray with flour; line bottom of pan with parchment paper.
3. In a large bowl, stir together gingersnap crumbs, melted butter, 2½ tablespoons sugar, and ¼ teaspoon salt until well combined. Using a straight-sided measuring cup, press crumb mixture into bottom and up sides of prepared pan.
4. Bake until set and fragrant, 8 to 10 minutes; let cool on a wire rack for 30 minutes. Wrap bottom and sides of pan in a double layer of heavy-duty foil.
5. Reduce oven temperature to 325°.
6. In the bowl of a stand mixer fitted with the paddle attachment, beat cream cheese and loose-leaf Earl Grey at medium speed until smooth and creamy, 2 to 3 minutes, stopping to scrape down sides of bowl. Add remaining 1½ cups sugar, flour, lemon zest, and remaining ¼ teaspoon salt; beat at low speed just until combined. Increase mixer speed to medium and beat until well combined, 1 to 2 minutes, stopping to scrape down sides of bowl. Add eggs, one at a time, beating just until combined after each addition. Add sour cream and chilled infused cream; beat at medium-low speed until well combined, 1 to 2 minutes, stopping to scrape down sides of bowl. Pour mixture into prepared crust.
7. Place pan in a large roasting pan. Carefully place roasting pan in oven and add hot water to a depth of 1 inch.
8. Bake until edges are set, top looks dry, center is almost set, and an instant-read thermometer inserted in center registers 150° to 155°, 1 hour 15 minutes to 1 hour 30 minutes. Let cool in pan on a wire rack for 1 hour and 30 minutes to 2 hours.
9. Refrigerate in pan on a wire rack overnight, loosely covering with foil to prevent condensation from forming on top of cheesecake. Run a knife around edges of cheesecake to release sides. Transfer to a serving plate. Use a warm dry knife to slice when ready to serve. Garnish with edible flowers and blueberries, if desired.

Talking about favorite reads over a dessert such as our Earl Grey Lemon Cheesecake is certain to sweeten the sharing of insights. This silken specialty leads our offering of a trio of desserts flavored with the classic tea blend.

For the light-as-air meringues of our Earl Grey Mini Pavlovas, very finely ground loose tea adds enchantment akin to a culinary fairy dust. Filling the shells is a pastry cream enhanced with fig preserves. Before nestling into this silken mixture, fresh fruit soaks overnight in an Earl Grey syrup that suffuses the tender orbs with delectable flavor. Find the recipe for our Earl Grey Rose Latte on page 21.

Earl Grey Mini Pavlovas

Makes 8 (4-inch) pavlovas

¼ cup **loose-leaf Earl Grey tea**, divided
7 **egg whites**, room temperature
2¾ cups **castor (superfine) sugar**, divided
1 tablespoon **cornstarch**
1½ teaspoons **white vinegar**
1 cup **water**
Fig Pastry Cream (recipe follows)
1 cup fresh **figs**, halved (approximately 9)

1. Preheat oven to 300°. Using a permanent marker and a 4-inch round cutter, draw 8 circles approximately 1 inch apart on parchment paper. Turn parchment over, and place on a baking sheet.
2. In the work bowl of a spice grinder, grind 2 tablespoons loose leaf Earl Grey tea until superfine.
3. In the bowl of a stand mixer fitted with the whisk attachment, beat egg whites at high speed until soft peaks form, about 1½ minutes. Gradually add 1¾ cups castor sugar, beating until mixture is glossy and sugar is dissolved, about 4 minutes. Turn off mixer. Lightly sift cornstarch over beaten egg whites, finely ground Earl Grey tea, and vinegar. Using a rubber spatula, fold cornstarch, tea, and vinegar into meringue.
4. Spoon 1 cup meringue inside each circle. Using a small offset spatula, form each portion until it is the width of the template drawn, with straight sides and a flat top, leaving a space in the center for ½ cup filling.
5. Place in oven and immediately reduce temperature to 225°. Bake until dry to the touch, about 1 hour and 10 minutes. Turn off oven and let meringues stand in oven with door closed for 8 hours or overnight.
6. In a medium saucepan, heat remaining 1 cup castor sugar, 1 cup water, and remaining 2 tablespoons Earl Grey tea until sugar is dissolved and mixture is fragrant and a deep brown color, 8 to 10 minutes. Strain through a fine-mesh sieve into a medium bowl. Add fresh figs, cover, and refrigerate overnight.
7. Before serving, spoon ½ cup Fig Pastry Cream into center of each pavlova. Top each pavlova with Earl Grey–soaked figs, and drizzle with additional Earl Grey syrup, if desired. Serve immediately.

Fig Pastry Cream

Makes approximately 4 cups

3 cups **whole milk**
1 cup **granulated sugar**, divided
8 **egg yolks**, room temperature
¼ cup plus 3 tablespoons **cornstarch**
¼ teaspoon **kosher salt**
¼ cup **unsalted butter**, softened
⅓ cup **fig preserves**

1. In a large saucepan, whisk together milk and ½ cup sugar. Heat over medium heat until steaming.
2. In a large bowl, whisk together egg yolks, cornstarch, salt, and remaining ½ cup sugar. Gradually add warm milk mixture to yolk mixture, whisking constantly. Pour mixture back into saucepan, and cook over medium heat, whisking constantly, until thickened and bubbly, 4 to 5 minutes. Boil until cornstarch flavor has cooked out, about 1 minute more.
3. Strain mixture through a fine-mesh sieve into a large bowl. Stir in softened butter in two additions. Cover with a piece of plastic wrap, pressing wrap directly onto surface of cream to prevent a skin from forming. Refrigerate until cold. Whisk in fig preserves until smooth before using.

Earl Grey Sticky Toffee Pudding Bundtlettes

Makes 6

4 **Earl Grey tea bags**
1 (6-ounce) package **pitted dates**
1⅓ cups **boiling water**
⅓ cup **butter**, softened
1 cup firmly packed **dark brown sugar**
2 large **eggs**, room temperature
1⅓ cups **self-rising flour**
1 teaspoon **vanilla extract**
Toffee Sauce (recipe follows)
Vanilla ice cream

1. Preheat oven to 350°.
2. In a medium bowl, combine tea bags, dates, and 1⅓ cups boiling water. Cover and let stand until dates have softened, approximately 30 minutes. (Do not drain.) Remove tea bags and pour date mixture into the container of a blender. Cover and blend until smooth.
3. In a large bowl, beat butter and brown sugar at medium speed with a mixer until fluffy, 3 to 4 minutes, stopping occasionally to scrape down sides of bowl. Add eggs, one at a time, beating well after each addition.
4. With mixer at low speed, add flour to butter mixture in thirds, alternately with date mixture, beginning and ending with flour. Add vanilla extract, beating to combine.
5. Spray 1 (6-well) Bundtlette baking pan with baking spray with flour. Fills wells approximately two-thirds full.
6. Bake until a wooden pick inserted near center comes out clean, 25 to 30 minutes. Remove from pans and trim bottoms so they are flat. Serve warm with Toffee Sauce and vanilla ice cream.

Toffee Sauce

Makes 1½ cups

½ cup **heavy whipping cream**, room temperature
2 **Earl Grey tea bags**
1 cup firmly packed **dark brown sugar**
½ cup **unsalted butter**, softened
½ teaspoon **kosher salt**

1. In a medium saucepan, heat cream over medium heat just until bubbles form around edges of pan (do not boil). Remove from heat and add tea bags; cover and let steep for 20 minutes. Remove tea bags, squeezing to extract as much liquid as possible.
2. In a medium saucepan, bring brown sugar and butter just to a boil over medium heat; reduce heat and simmer, whisking until sugar is fully dissolved, 3 to 5 minutes. Add infused cream and salt. Whisk mixture until cream is fully incorporated and beginning to simmer, about 3 minutes. Serve warm.

CHILDHOOD TREASURES

There's an enduring magic to teatimes inspired by literature that shaped one's early years. Hearts soar while encountering favorite characters and revisiting faraway lands. Storybook settings paired with treats that pay homage to cherished tales make such occasions even more enjoyable.

The Secret Garden in NEW YORK CITY

Amidst Manhattan's concrete jungle, Central Park is a sprawling, verdant refuge where urban life melts away. Here, a secluded alcove honors beloved children's author Frances Hodgson Burnett and her famous tale.

In the southern section of the park's Conservatory Garden, an English-style oasis twists and turns with wild whimsy. At its center is a pool dotted with water lilies and a bronze fountain said to depict Mary and Dickon from The Secret Garden.

After the British-American author's death in 1924, her admirers found the perfect place for a memorial: a blooming garden. The square's centerpiece, sculpted by Bessie Potter Vonnoh, is shaded by the oldest crab apple tree in the park and can be reached by a series of winding paths, beginning at the famous Vanderbilt Gate. For generations, lovers of literature have gathered in this haven, perhaps seeking the sort of rejuvenation experienced by the characters of Burnett's cherished novel.

"I AM WRITING IN THE GARDEN. TO WRITE AS ONE SHOULD OF A GARDEN ONE MUST WRITE NOT OUTSIDE IT OR MERELY SOMEWHERE NEAR IT, BUT IN THE GARDEN."

—Frances Hodgson Burnett

RASPBERRY SOCIAL

Taking inspiration from the bevy of sweets mentioned in Lucy Maud Montgomery's Anne of Green Gables series, we offer a menu of recipes bursting with brilliant red fruit.

Above left: In central character Anne Shirley's early days as a teacher, she receives an irresistible invitation: "'Of course I'll stay to tea,' said Anne gaily. 'I was dying to be asked. My mouth has been watering for some more of your grandma's delicious shortbread.'" In tribute to Mrs. Irving's tempting specialty, we present our recipe for Raspberry Shortbread Creams.

Above right: Delight continues in Raspberry White Chocolate Tart, a treat Anne might have shared while a pupil at Avonlea School. Opposite: Topping our tiered server are Pink Heart Candies, confections reminiscent of a romantic gesture made by Gilbert Blythe in Anne of Green Gables.

Along with hot tea, which figures prominently in L. M. Montgomery's series, another beverage that stands out is the concoction of raspberries, sugar, and lemon juice that Anne enjoys after a church social. Above left: We present refreshing Raspberry Cordial alongside Gin-Cordial Cocktail, which adds spirits to the classic drink.

Above right: Described as "light and white" in the books, "baking-powder biscuits" find a tasty alternative in our berry-topped Ruby Rose Tea Biscuits. Below left: Recalling a baking disaster—"'Oh, Marilla,' sobbed Anne, without looking up, 'I'm disgraced forever. ... I shall always be pointed at as the girl who flavored a cake with anodyne liniment'"—we perfect the recipe for Lemon Layer Cake.

RECIPES

Pink Heart Candies

Makes 24

2 cups **marshmallow fluff**
9 tablespoons finely ground **freeze-dried raspberries**, divided
1 tablespoon solid **coconut oil**, melted
1 (10-ounce) package white vanilla-flavored **candy coating**

1. In a small bowl, stir together marshmallow fluff and 8 tablespoons freeze-dried raspberry powder until well combined. Transfer mixture to a pipping bag fitted with a ½-inch round piping tip. Set aside.
2. In a small bowl, combine melted coconut oil and remaining 1 tablespoon raspberry powder.
3. In a small bowl set on top of a double boiler, melt candy coating over simmering water. Remove bowl from heat and stir in coconut-raspberry mixture.
4. Pour melted candy into heart-shaped chocolate moulds, tapping gently to release air bubbles. Flip moulds over and let excess candy drain back into bowl. Using a bench scraper or offset metal spatula, scrape excess coating from top of moulds. Refrigerate to set, about 10 minutes. Repeat process once more.
5. Remove moulds from refrigerator and fill with marshmallow mixture to approximately ⅛ inch from top. Freeze for 10 minutes.
6. Return small bowl to top of double boiler and melt remaining candy.
7. Remove moulds from freezer and fill to the top with melted candy. Using a bench scraper or offset spatula, scrape to create a clean edge. Freeze for 10 minutes more.
8. Invert moulds to release candies. Let candies come to room temperature before serving. Store in an airtight container for up to 2 weeks.

Raspberry Shortbread Creams

Makes 12 sandwich cookies

½ cup **unsalted butter**, softened
½ cup **granulated sugar**
1 **egg yolk**, room temperature
⅓ cup **condensed milk**
2 teaspoons **vanilla extract**
1⅔ cups **all-purpose flour**
2 tablespoons finely ground **freeze-dried raspberries**
1 tablespoon **white rice flour**
¾ teaspoon **kosher salt**
½ teaspoon **baking powder**
¼ teaspoon **baking soda**
4 to 6 drops **red gel food coloring**
Vanilla Buttercream (recipe follows)
¼ cup **raspberry jam**

1. In the bowl of a stand mixer fitted with the paddle attachment, beat butter and sugar at medium speed until fluffy, 3 to 4 minutes, stopping to scrape down sides of bowl. Add egg yolk, beating well after each addition. Add condensed milk and vanilla extract, beating just until combined.
2. In a medium bowl, whisk together flour, ground raspberries, rice flour, salt, baking powder, and baking soda.
3. With mixer at low speed, gradually add flour mixture to butter mixture, beating just until combined. Add in food coloring and beat until just combined. Cover tightly with plastic wrap; refrigerate for 1 hour.
4. Preheat oven to 300°. Place oven rack in lower third of oven. Line 2 large rimmed baking sheets with parchment paper.
5. On a lightly floured surface, roll disk to ¼-inch thickness. Using a 2½-inch fluted round cutter, cut dough. Place 2 inches apart on prepared pans.
6. Bake until tops are dry, 15 to 20 minutes. Let cool on pans for 5 minutes. Remove from pans and let cool completely on wire racks.
7. Spoon Vanilla Buttercream into a piping bag fitted with a ¼-inch French-star piping tip*. Pipe a border of buttercream onto flat side of half of cookies. Spoon raspberry jam into a piping bag; cut a ¼-inch tip on the end. Fill center of buttercream border with raspberry jam. Gently place remaining cookies, flat side down, on top of filling. Carefully press sandwich cookies together (use light pressure to prevent cracking). Cookies are best served the same day. Store in an airtight container at room temperature for up to 3 days.

**We used an Ateco #862 decorating tip.*

Vanilla Buttercream

Makes approximately 2 cups

1 cup **unsalted butter**, softened
4 cups **confectioners' sugar**
2 tablespoons **heavy whipping cream**
1 teaspoon **vanilla extract**
¼ teaspoon **kosher salt**

In the bowl of a stand mixer fitted with the paddle attachment, beat butter at medium speed until creamy, 5 to 6 minutes. Gradually add confectioners' sugar, beating until combined. Add cream, vanilla extract, and salt, beating until smooth.

Raspberry White Chocolate Tart

Makes 1 (13½x4¼-inch) tart

2¼ cups **whole milk**
⅓ cup plus 2 tablespoons **granulated sugar**, divided
3 **egg yolks**
4 tablespoons **cornstarch**
1 teaspoon **kosher salt**
1 tablespoon **vanilla extract**
2 tablespoons **unsalted butter**, room temperature
4 ounces **white chocolate**, finely chopped
Pâte Sablée Crust (recipe follows)
6 tablespoons warm **seedless raspberry jam**, warmed (see Note)
Fresh **raspberries**
Garnish: fresh **mint**

1. In a large saucepan, whisk together milk and ⅓ cup sugar. Heat over medium heat until steaming.
2. In a large bowl, whisk together egg yolks, cornstarch, salt, and remaining 2 tablespoons sugar. Gradually add warm milk mixture to egg mixture, whisking constantly. Pour mixture back into saucepan and cook over medium heat, whisking constantly, until thickened and boiling, 4 to 5 minutes. Add vanilla extract and whisk until well combined. Strain mixture through a fine-mesh sieve into a large heatproof bowl. Stir in butter and white chocolate.
3. Spoon into Pâte Sablée Crust and cover with a piece of plastic wrap, pressing wrap directly onto surface of pastry cream to prevent a skin from forming. Refrigerate until cooled and completely set.
4. Spread raspberry jam over filling and top with raspberries; brush raspberries lightly with any remaining jam. Garnish with mint, if desired.

Note: Thin raspberry jam with 1 to 2 teaspoons of water, if needed.

Pâte Sablée Crust

1 cup **unsalted butter**, softened
⅔ cup **confectioners' sugar**
2 teaspoons **lemon zest**
1 teaspoon **kosher salt**
2 **egg yolks**
½ teaspoon **vanilla extract**
3 cups **pastry flour**

1. In the bowl of a stand mixer fitted with the paddle attachment, beat butter at medium speed until smooth, about 1 minute. Add confectioners' sugar, lemon zest, and salt; beat until smooth, about 1 minute. Add egg yolks and vanilla extract; beat until combined, about 1 minute. Add flour in two additions, beating just until combined.
2. Turn out dough onto a lightly floured surface and gently knead 3 to 4 times. Shape dough into a 5-inch square and wrap in plastic wrap. Refrigerate for 1 hour.
3. Preheat oven to 325°.
4. On a lightly floured surface, roll dough into an 16x6-inch rectangle, approximately ¼-inch thick. Transfer to a 13½x4¼-inch rectangular tart pan, gently pressing into bottom and completely up sides. Trim excess dough. Freeze until hardened, about 10 minutes.
5. Top dough with a piece of parchment paper, letting ends extend over edges of pan. Add pie weights.
6. Bake until edges are light golden brown, about 30 minutes. Carefully remove paper and weights. Bake until crust is golden brown, about 10 minutes more. Let cool completely on a wire rack.

Ruby Rose Tea Biscuits

Makes 9

2 cups **all-purpose flour**
4 teaspoons **baking powder**
1 tablespoon **granulated sugar**
½ teaspoon **fine sea salt**
½ cup cold **unsalted butter**, grated
¾ cup **whole milk**
2 tablespoons **Raspberry Jam** (recipe follows)
9 fresh **raspberries**
Rose Cream (recipe follows)

1. Preheat oven to 425°. Line a rimmed baking sheet with parchment paper.
2. In a large bowl, whisk together flour, baking powder, sugar, and salt. Stir in butter and mix until mixture resembles coarse crumbs. Add milk and stir until just combined.
3. Turn out dough onto a lightly floured surface and knead until a smooth dough forms. Pat into a ½-inch-thick rectangle. Using a 2¼-inch round cutter dipped in flour, cut 9 biscuits, rerolling scraps once, and place on prepared baking sheet.
4. Dip a finger in flour and press a deep well into the top of each biscuit. Spoon a heaping ½ teaspoon Raspberry Jam into each well. Freeze until firm, about 15 minutes.
5. Bake until golden brown and puffed, 10 to 12 minutes. Top each with a raspberry and serve with Raspberry Jam and Rose Cream.

Raspberry Jam

Makes 3 cups or 1 cup seedless

6 cups fresh **raspberries**
4 cups **granulated sugar**
2 tablespoons **lemon juice**

Place raspberries in a medium pot and mash with a spoon. Heat over medium heat until softened, 7 to 10 minutes. Stir in sugar and lemon juice. Cook over medium heat, stirring frequently, until thickened and bubbly and a candy thermometer registers 220°, 35 to 40 minutes. Strain through a fine-mesh sieve and discard seeds, if desired. Let cool completely. Transfer to an airtight container. Refrigerate up to 1 week.

Rose Cream
Makes 1½ cups

½ cup **heavy whipping cream**
1 tablespoon crushed **organic dried rose petals**
1 teaspoon **granulated sugar**
½ cup **mascarpone**
Garnish: **organic dried rose petals**

1. In a small saucepan, heat cream and rose petals over medium heat until steaming (do not boil). Remove from heat and let cool completely. Strain and refrigerate until cold, about 30 minutes.
2. In the bowl of a stand mixer fitted with the whisk attachment, beat cream and sugar until stiff peaks form. Fold in mascarpone. Garnish with dried rose petals, if desired.

Raspberry Cordial
Makes 2 cups

3 (6-ounce) packages fresh **raspberries**
1 cup **granulated sugar**
1 cup **water**
2 tablespoons **white balsamic vinegar**
2 tablespoons **lemon juice**

In a medium saucepan, combine raspberries, sugar, 1 cup water, vinegar, and lemon juice. Heat over medium heat until raspberries are very soft, 10 to 15 minutes. Remove from heat and let cool to room temperature. Strain mixture through a fine-mesh sieve and discard solids. Transfer to an airtight container and refrigerate until chilled or up to 2 weeks.

Gin-Cordial Cocktail
Makes 1

3 ounces **Raspberry Cordial** (recipe above)
1½ ounces **gin**
¼ ounce **lime juice**
Sparkling water, to serve
Garnish: **lemon peel**

Fill glass with ice. Add Raspberry Cordial, gin, and lime juice. Top with sparkling water. Garnish with lemon peel, if desired.

Lemon Layer Cake
Make 1 (8-inch) Cake

1½ cups **unsalted butter**, softened
3 cups **granulated sugar**
3 tablespoons **lemon zest**
4 large **eggs**, room temperature
1½ teaspoons **vanilla extract**
4½ cups **all-purpose flour**
1 tablespoon **baking powder**
1¼ teaspoons **kosher salt**
¼ teaspoon **baking soda**
1¾ cups **buttermilk**, room temperature
White Chocolate Buttercream (recipe follows)
½ cup **lemon curd**
½ cup **seedless raspberry jam**
Garnish: fresh **raspberries, lemon peel twists**

1. Preheat oven to 350°. Spray 3 (8-inch) round cake pans with baking spray with flour. Line bottom of pans with parchment paper.
2. In the bowl of a stand mixer fitted with the paddle attachment, beat butter, sugar, and lemon zest at medium speed until fluffy, stopping to scrape down sides of bowl. Add eggs, one at a time, beating well after each addition. Beat in vanilla extract.
3. In a medium bowl, stir together flour, baking powder, salt, and baking soda. With mixer at low speed, gradually add flour mixture to butter mixture, alternately with buttermilk, beginning and ending with flour mixture, beating just until combined after each addition. Divide among prepared pans.
4. Bake until a wooden pick inserted in centers comes out clean, 35 to 40 minutes. Let cool in pans for 10 minutes. Remove from pans and let cool completely on wire racks. Level cakes, if desired.
5. Place one layer onto cake plate; spread a thin layer of White Chocolate Buttercream over top. Spoon 1 cup of buttercream into a piping bag. Cut a ¼-inch hole at the end and pipe a small border around the edge of the layer to create a dam. Spread ¼ cup lemon curd and then ¼ cup raspberry jam within the buttercream dam. Repeat with next layer of cake. Top with remaining layer and spread buttercream over top and sides of cake. Garnish with raspberries and lemon peel twists, if desired.

White Chocolate Buttercream

3 cups **unsalted butter**, softened
8 cups **confectioners' sugar**
2 teaspoons **kosher salt**
1 tablespoon **vanilla extract**
8 ounces **white chocolate**, melted and cooled

In the bowl of a stand mixer fitted with the paddle attachment, beat butter at medium-low speed until soft, about 1 minute. Add in confectioners' sugar, 1 cup at a time, and beat until well combined. Beat in salt, vanilla extract, and white chocolate until well combined. Increase speed to high and beat mixture until smooth and well combined, 1 to 2 minutes.

"'THAT'S AWFULLY NICE RASPBERRY CORDIAL, ANNE,' SHE SAID. 'I DIDN'T KNOW RASPBERRY CORDIAL WAS SO NICE.'"

—L. M. Montgomery

TO NORTH POLE
BIG STONES AND ROX
NICE FOR PIKNICKS
BEE TREE
SANDY PIT WHERE ROO PLAYS
RABBITS HOUSE
RABBITS FRIENDS AND RALETIONS
MY HOUSE
SIX PINE TREES
OWLS HOUSE
POOH TRAP FOR HEFFALUMPS
100 AKER WOOD
EEYORES GLOOMY PLACE
BY ME AND MR SHEPARD HELPD
MR SANDERS
A.A. MILNE

Tea with CHRISTOPHER ROBIN

The year 2025 marked the 100th anniversary of When We Were Young, *English author A. A. Milne's best-selling book of poetry that gives the first reference to Winnie-the-Pooh. To celebrate more than a century of the beloved bear, we offer a teatime menu that evokes nostalgic recollections of the Hundred Acre Wood.*

Over steaming cups of tea, venture with Victoria *to the fictional land of teddy bear Winnie-the-Pooh and friends, a coterie of lovable characters developed by A. A. Milne. The writer based the young boy at the center of the tales on his son, Christopher Robin Milne. For this feature, we escape to memories of childhood story times to linger over an alfresco repast. The party begins with individually portioned servings of Butternut Squash Soup, opposite, and continues with a colorful selection of tasty Vegetable Garden Open-Faced Tea Sandwiches, this page, below left.*

Opposite: Woodland Berry Scones are certain to be appreciated, especially when served with Whipped Honey. This page, clockwise from below right: "A day without a friend," Winnie-the-Pooh muses to Piglet, "is like a pot without a single drop of honey left inside." This afternoon tea promises generous helpings of both treasures, with silken Salted Honey Pots de Crème divided among ramekins for cherished guests. Baked until set, the custards are crowned with honeycomb and edible blooms. Mini Carrot Cakes, topped with a tinted swirl of cream cheese frosting and dainty sprigs of green, offer a sweet nod to Rabbit. Wildflower White Chocolate Bark tempts with a smattering of pistachios, petals, and peppercorns sprinkled over bittersweet and white chocolate.

RECIPES

Vegetable Garden Open-Faced Tea Sandwiches

Makes 24

6 slices **pumpernickel rye bread**, lightly toasted
4 ounces **cream cheese**, softened
1 (5.2-ounce) package **herbed cheese spread**, softened
2 tablespoons sliced fresh **chives**
1 tablespoon chopped fresh **dill**
¼ cup shaved **carrots**
¼ cup thinly sliced **Persian cucumber**
¼ cup shaved **golden beet**
¼ cup shaved **radish**
1 tablespoon **olive oil**
Flaky sea salt
Garnish: **micro greens**

1. Preheat oven to 375°. Line a rimmed baking sheet with parchment paper.
2. Using a sharp knife, cut each slice of bread into 2½-inch squares, discarding crusts or saving for another use. Cut each square in half diagonally to make 2 triangles. Place on prepared pan. Bake until lightly toasted, 7 to 10 minutes.
3. In a small bowl, beat cream cheese, herbed cheese spread, chives, and dill with a mixer at low speed until smooth.
4. Transfer to a piping bag. Cut a ¼-inch opening at the tip of the piping bag. Pipe cream cheese mixture onto toasts. Arrange shaved vegetables on triangles, as desired. Drizzle with olive oil and sprinkle with flaky sea salt. Garnish with micro greens, if desired.

Butternut Squash Soup

Makes approximately 12 (2-ounce) servings

2 tablespoons **unsalted butter**
½ cup finely chopped **yellow onion**
½ cup finely chopped **celery**
2 cloves **garlic**, minced
2 teaspoons minced fresh **ginger**
4 cups diced **butternut squash**
1 teaspoon **kosher salt**
1 teaspoon **smoked paprika**
1 teaspoon ground **turmeric**
3 cups **vegetable broth**
1 cup whole fat **coconut milk**, plus more for topping
Toasted pine nuts, to serve
Garnish: **smoked paprika**, **celery leaves**

1. In a large pot or Dutch oven, melt butter over medium heat. Add onion, celery, garlic, and ginger; cook, stirring occasionally, until softened and translucent, 5 to 7 minutes. Stir in butternut squash, salt, smoked paprika, and turmeric; cook 5 minutes more.
2. Stir in vegetable broth; bring to a boil. Reduce to a simmer and cook, stirring occasionally, until squash is very tender, 15 to 20 minutes. Stir in coconut milk.
3. Working in batches, if necessary, transfer soup to the container of a blender; remove center piece of lid to let steam escape and place a clean towel over opening in lid to avoid splatters. Process until smooth.
4. Divide soup among desired glasses. Top with coconut milk and toasted pine nuts. Garnish with smoked paprika and celery leaves, if desired.

Woodland Berry Scones with Whipped Honey

Makes 12 scones

2 cups **all-purpose flour**
6 tablespoons **granulated sugar**, divided
1 tablespoon **baking powder**
2 teaspoons **kosher salt**
1 teaspoon ground **cardamom**
5 tablespoons cold **unsalted butter**, cubed
¼ cup fresh **raspberries**, frozen
¼ cup fresh **blackberries**, halved and frozen
¼ cup fresh **blueberries**, frozen
¼ cup diced **strawberries**, frozen (¼-inch pieces)
1 cup plus 1 tablespoon **heavy whipping cream**, divided
Whipped Honey (recipe follows)

1. Preheat oven to 425°. Line a baking sheet with parchment paper.
2. In the work bowl of a food processor, place flour, 3 tablespoons granulated sugar, baking powder, kosher salt, and cardamom; pulse until combined. Add cold butter and pulse until mixture is crumbly.
3. Transfer flour mixture to a large bowl. Add raspberries, blackberries, blueberries, and strawberries; toss to coat. Gently fold in 1 cup cream, stirring until combined. Turn out dough onto a lightly floured surface, and gently knead, just until dough comes together. Shape dough into 2 (1-inch-thick) disks and cut each into 6 wedges. Place 1 inch apart on prepared pan. Freeze until firm, about 15 minutes.
4. Brush tops of scones with remaining 1 tablespoon cream. Bake until golden brown, 12 to 15 minutes. Sprinkle with remaining 3 tablespoons granulated sugar. Serve with Whipped Honey.

Whipped Honey

Makes 1 cup

1 cup raw **honey**

In the bowl of a stand mixer fitted with the paddle attachment, beat honey at high speed until very pale in color, about 10 minutes. Transfer to an airtight container and store in a cool, dry, dark place.

Wildflower White Chocolate Bark

Makes 12 servings

2 (4-ounce) bars **bittersweet chocolate**
3 (4-ounce) bars **white chocolate**, chopped
¼ cup slivered **pistachios**
2 tablespoons edible **dried wildflower petals**
1 teaspoon ground **pink peppercorns**

1. Line a 9x13-inch rimmed baking sheet with parchment paper. Place bittersweet chocolate in a medium heatproof bowl. Place white chocolate in a separate medium heatproof bowl.
2. Fill a medium saucepan with water to a depth of 1 inch. Bring to a boil over medium-high heat. Reduce heat to low and place the bowl of bittersweet chocolate on top. Heat, stirring occasionally, until mixture is melted, 5 to 8 minutes. Pour into prepared pan and spread in an even layer. Refrigerate until set and dry, 15 to 20 minutes.
3. Place bowl of white chocolate on top of pot and heat, stirring occasionally, until melted and smooth, 5 to 8 minutes. Spread melted white chocolate in an even layer on top of bittersweet chocolate, careful not to mix bittersweet chocolate into white chocolate. Sprinkle with pistachios, dried wildflower petals, and pink peppercorns. Let cool completely. Break into pieces.

Salted Honey Pots de Crème

Makes 12

2½ cups **heavy whipping cream**
⅔ cup **whole milk**
¾ cup **honey**, divided
½ teaspoon **kosher salt**
6 large **egg yolks**
4 teaspoons **vanilla extract**, divided
Garnish: **honeycomb**, **edible flowers**

1. Preheat oven to 300°. Line a 9x13-inch deep baking dish with a damp towel. Place 12 (4-ounce) ovenproof ramekins in prepared pan.
2. In a medium saucepan, heat cream, milk, ½ cup honey, and salt over medium-low heat until honey is dissolved and mixture is steaming, 10 to 12 minutes (do not boil).
3. In a large bowl, whisk egg yolks until slightly fluffy and lightened in color, 1 to 2 minutes. While whisking constantly, gradually add half of cream mixture to egg mixture, ¼ cup at a time, until fully combined. Add remaining half of cream mixture and 2 teaspoons vanilla extract, whisking to combine. Divide mixture among prepared ramekins. (Tip: If there are air bubbles on top of mixture, using a kitchen torch, gently torch tops just until bubbles dissipate.)
4. In a medium saucepan, bring 5 cups water to a boil over high heat. Pour enough hot water into baking dish to come halfway up sides of ramekins.
5. Bake until edges of custards are set, 50 to 55 minutes. Let cool completely in pan. Remove from pan and cover with plastic wrap. Refrigerate until chilled, at least 4 hours or up to overnight.
6. In a small bowl, combine remaining ¼ cup honey and remaining 2 teaspoons vanilla extract. Just before serving, divide mixture among ramekins. Garnish with honeycomb and edible flowers, if desired.

Mini Carrot Cakes

Makes 12

2 cups **all-purpose flour**
1½ teaspoons **baking powder**
½ teaspoon **kosher salt**
½ teaspoon ground **cinnamon**
½ teaspoon ground **ginger**
1½ cups firmly packed **light brown sugar**
¾ cup **vegetable oil**
½ cup **unsweetened apple sauce**
2 large **eggs**
2 teaspoons **vanilla extract**
1½ cups grated **carrot**, tops reserved
2 tablespoons chopped **crystalized ginger**
Cream Cheese Frosting (recipe follows)
Orange food coloring

1. Preheat oven to 350°. Spray an 18x13-inch baking sheet with baking spray with flour. Line with parchment paper. Spray parchment with baking spray with flour.
2. In a large bowl, whisk together flour, baking powder, kosher salt, cinnamon, and ground ginger.
3. In a separate large bowl, whisk together brown sugar, oil, apple sauce, eggs, and vanilla extract. Gradually whisk dry ingredients into wet ingredients. Fold in carrots and crystalized ginger. Spread batter into prepared pan.
4. Bake until a wooden pick inserted in center comes out clean, 20 to 30 minutes. Let cool for 15 minutes. Turn cake out onto a wire rack and let cool completely.
5. Place ¼ cup Cream Cheese Frosting in a small bowl. Add desired amount of food coloring; stir until well combined. Spread remaining cream cheese frosting on top of cake. Freeze until very firm, about 30 minutes (or refrigerate for 2 hours).
6. Using a 2½-inch round cutter, cut cake into 24 rounds. Discard scraps or save for another use. Carefully stack 1 round on top of another. Repeat with remaining rounds to get 12 mini cakes.
7. Transfer orange frosting to a piping bag fitted with a small round piping tip*. Pipe carrots onto tops of cakes. Just before serving, divide carrot tops among cakes.

**We used a Wilton No. 7 decorating tip.*

Cream Cheese Frosting

Makes 3 cups

8 ounces **cream cheese**, softened
½ cup **unsalted butter**, softened
1 teaspoon **vanilla extract**
½ teaspoon **kosher salt**
4 cups **confectioners' sugar**

In the bowl of a stand mixer fitted with the paddle attachment, beat cream cheese at medium speed until smooth. Add butter and beat until creamy. Beat in vanilla extract and salt until combined. Gradually add confectioners' sugar, beating until smooth.

THE LEGACY OF BEATRIX POTTER

A celebrated author known for her petite tomes filled with charming stories and watercolor illustrations, Beatrix Potter's talents and interests extended widely beyond children's literature. An avid farmer, she coupled this love with a vision for conservation—becoming an active force in the preservation of the Lake District in England. Her heritage lives on in the northwest region of Cumbria.

Raised in London, the noted author and artist Beatrix Potter was captivated by England's Lake District during her childhood holidays spent among the quaint hamlets and misty moors. As a girl, she collected small animals during these trips and gently tamed them into pets. The domesticated creatures provided inspiration and companionship during her solitary Victorian childhood as she developed her story-writing and artistic talents. When Beatrix grew into adulthood, these tales and illustrations were published, and the now-cherished books became her livelihood. She continued to use many of the landscapes and villages of the Lake District as the backdrops for her woodland animal characters.

In addition to her literary fame, Beatrix was well known for her dedication to farming and the community. She used the profits from her first book to buy Hill Top, a seventeenth-century cottage and garden in the town of Near Sawrey, in 1905. Although still living in London, the author escaped to the Lake District as often as possible, immersing herself in bucolic farm life and enjoying the waterside lifestyle. Beatrix continued her creative endeavors, writing and illustrating books about the animals she so loved. Her affinity for agriculture and livestock served as both a means of living and a muse, as she painted her flock of sheep and the naughty rabbits that came to nibble at her garden's edge.

Following the death of her first fiancé, publisher Norman Warne, Beatrix relocated to the Lake District, working year-round at Hill Top and later marrying William Heelis, a local solicitor who advised her in purchasing cottages and land parcels within the area. Mrs. Heelis, as she was known locally, became an ardent conservationist and a Herdwick sheep farmer. Her agrarian pursuits developed into award-winning farming practices and a devout desire to preserve the rural way of life. Utilizing her intellect and passion, she grew to become an astute businesswoman and inspirational farmer.

With an inheritance from her family and the profits from her books, she acquired land throughout the Cumbrian region. Longstanding friendship with Canon Rawnsley, one of the founding members of the British National Trust, led Beatrix to leave fourteen farms and more than 4,000 acres to the institution upon her death, thus ensuring the preservation of a way of life and the beauty of her beloved lakeside landscape for generations to come.

Blackberry Gin and Tonic

1 cocktail

2 ounces **gin**
¾ ounce freshly squeezed **lime juice**
½ ounce **Cucumber Simple Syrup** (recipe follows)
Crushed ice
5 to 6 fresh **blackberries**
2 slices **cucumber**
4 ounces **tonic water**
Garnish: shaved or sliced **mini cucumber**, fresh **blackberries**, **lime slices**

1. In a cocktail shaker, add gin, lime juice, and Cucumber Simple Syrup. Add ice. Cover and shake until cold, 10 to 15 seconds.
2. In the bottom of a serving glass, muddle blackberries and cucumber slices. Pour gin mixture over mashed berries mixture. Add ice to fill and top with tonic water. Garnish with cucumber strips or slices, blackberries, and lime slices, if desired.

Cucumber Simple Syrup

Makes ⅓ cup

2 cucumber peels*
½ cup seeded and chopped **cucumber**
½ cup **granulated sugar**
½ cup **water**
Peel from **1 lime**

In a small saucepan, bring cucumber peels, chopped cucumber, sugar, water, and lime peels to a boil over medium heat. Continue to boil for 10 minutes. Remove from heat and let cool completely. Strain mixture through a fine-mesh sieve into an airtight container, discarding solids. Refrigerate for up to 2 weeks.

**We used mini cucumbers.*

Author and illustrator Beatrix Potter was also a noted naturalist whose Lake District property included a higgledy-piggledy cottage garden. Our recipes draw inspiration from the half-acre she lovingly tended. Blackberry Gin and Tonic, this page, pays tribute to fruit that characters Flopsy, Mopsy, and Peter Cottontail enjoyed for supper. Individually portioned Carrot Soufflé, page 76, includes an organic bloom as a nod to Beatrix's observation: "The flowers love the house, they try to come in! House leek grows on the window sills and ledges; wisteria climbs the wall, clematis chokes the spout casings ... But nothing more sweet than the old pink cabbage rose that peeps in at the small paned windows."

Carrot Soufflé

Makes 6 servings

2 pounds peeled **carrots**, chopped
1 teaspoon **kosher salt**, divided
½ cup **unsalted butter**, diced
¼ cup **all-purpose flour**
1 teaspoon **baking powder**
½ cup **granulated sugar**
¼ cup firmly packed **light brown sugar**
2 teaspoons **orange zest**
½ teaspoon ground **cinnamon**
½ teaspoon ground **ginger**
¼ teaspoon ground **nutmeg**
1 teaspoon **vanilla extract**
3 large **eggs**, lightly beaten
Garnish: **confectioners' sugar, edible flowers***

1. Preheat oven to 350°. Lightly butter 6 (¾-cup) soufflé dishes or ramekins, and place on a rimmed baking sheet.
2. In a 3-quart saucepan, place carrots and cover with water; add ½ teaspoon salt. Bring to a boil over medium-high heat; reduce heat to medium and cook until fork tender, about 20 minutes.
3. Drain carrots and transfer half to the container of a blender. Add butter and top with remaining half of carrots. Process until smooth, stopping once or twice to stir.
4. To blender container, add flour, baking powder, granulated sugar, brown sugar, orange zest, cinnamon, ginger, remaining ½ teaspoon salt, nutmeg, vanilla extract, and eggs. Purée until fluffy and smooth, stopping to stir occasionally. Spoon evenly into prepared dishes.
5. Bake, uncovered, until puffed and lightly browned, about 35 minutes. Serve warm. Just before serving, garnish with a dusting of confectioners' sugar and edible flowers, if desired.

**We used flowers from Gourmet Sweet Botanicals, gourmetsweetbotanicals.com.*

BRITISH SOJOURNS

Journey to a nation steeped in ardor for both the written word and refined refreshment. From a village brimming with booksellers and a tearoom tucked inside a library to destinations associated with a beloved novelist, a multitude of bliss awaits discovery in Britain.

Pages Past & PRESENT

Nestled along the southeast bank of the River Wye in Wales, just a stone's throw from the English border, lies a flourishing community where reading isn't simply a pleasant pastime but the signature business.

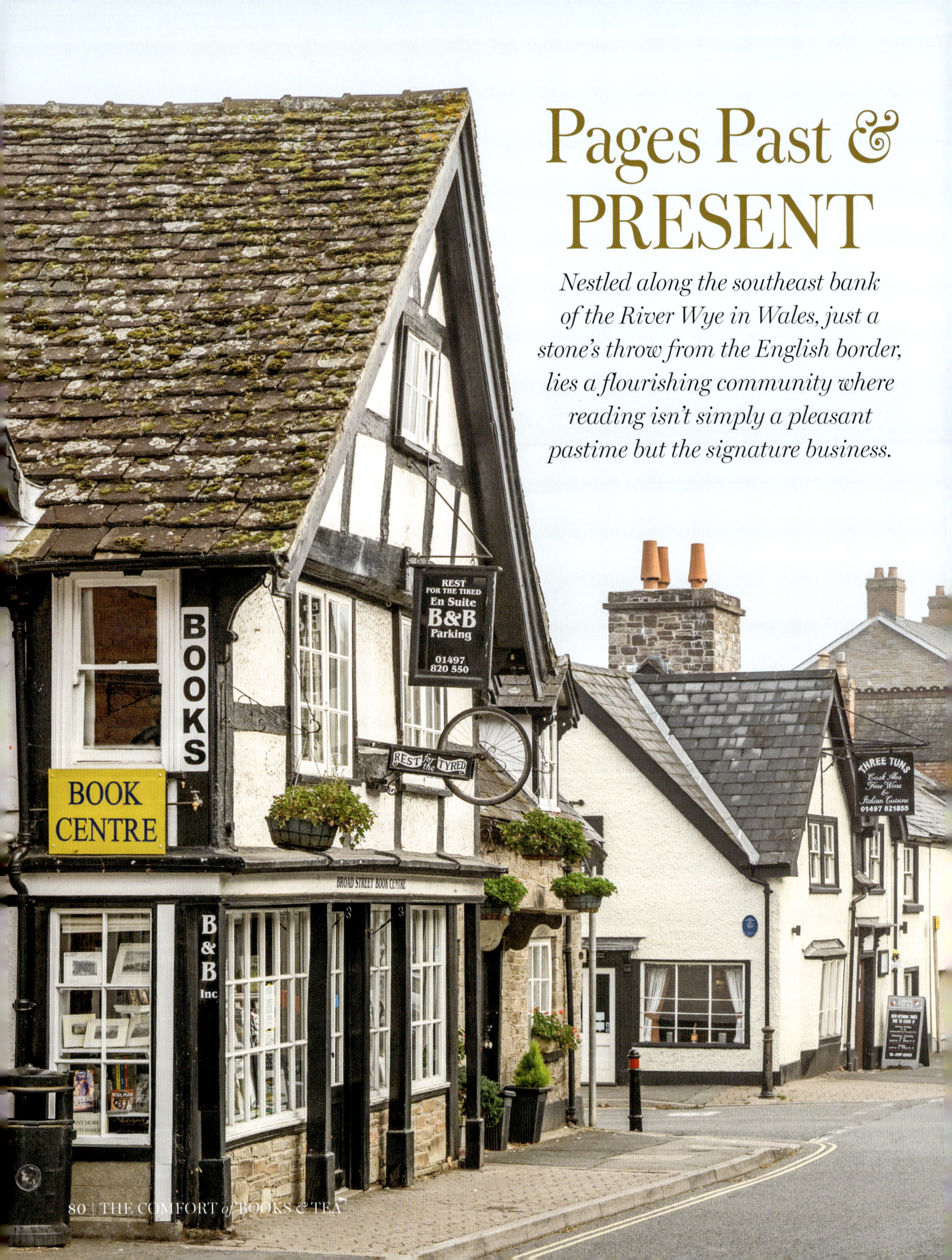

When Richard Booth opened his first bookstore in 1962, Hay-on-Wye was a twelfth-century market town with a waning city center. The eccentric entrepreneur was determined that Hay would not go the way of so many small villages, where large conglomerates drew customers away from long-established local shops. To that end, Booth—along with a contingency of stalwart men from Hay—set out on a book-buying expedition across America, purchasing thousands upon thousands of second-hand volumes from libraries and shipping them back across the pond in crates.

In the ensuing years, Hay became known as "The Town of Books," boasting more than two dozen booksellers, each carrying a cornucopia of new and used volumes. Booth achieved his original purpose; Hay became an alluring destination for bibliophiles who converged on the community, filling its coffers with tourist dollars and shoring up its flagging economy. The annual Hay Festival, celebrating the town's claim to fame, is a much-attended event, where patrons mingle among authors and poets, historians, and musicians.

But beyond the books and assorted shops, this picturesque part of Wales begs exploration. Hay's architecture is stunning—especially St. Mary's Church and medieval fortress Hay Castle—and the breathtaking landscape surrounding the hamlet is perfect for both casual strolls and ambitious hikes. Richard Booth's modern-day vision for Hay-on-Wye blends beautifully with the burg's ancient history, playing out amid the stories, stones, and steadfast current of the River Wye, beckoning visitors to partake of all the page-turning pleasures this extraordinary town has to offer.

TRADER HORN
TWENTY-FIVE
GREY WOLF
JURGEN
SOUTH WIND

STIMSON'S REEF
STANLEY AND AFRICA
WALTER SCOTT
TALES FROM HAKLUYT
FRANK ELIAS
BLACK
SCHÖNBERG-COTTA FAMILY
NELSON
MRS. O.F. WALTON
MR MIDSHIPMAN EASY
CAPTAIN MARRYAT
DONE AND DARED IN OLD FRANCE
DEBORAH ALCOCK
PARTRIDGE
IN THE KING'S SERVICE
CAPT F. S. BRERETON
OLD RED SCHOOL HOUSE
JAMES LUMSDEN
SEA-DOGS ALL!
T. BEVAN
NELSON
EVERYDAY HEROES
QUEEN MAB
SPCK
ROMANCE OF REAL LIFE
EAST LYNNE
UNDER THREE KINGS
TWO LITTLE CAVALIERS
NELSON
ERIC OR LITTLE BY LITTLE
FARRAR
UNCLE TOM'S CABIN
HELEN MORDAUNT
UNDER HAIG IN FLANDERS
IN THE EASTERN SEAS
KINGSTON
NELSON
TRAFALGAR REFOUGHT
SIR W. LAIRD CLOWES & ALAN H. BURGOYNE
NELSON
CHARLES KINGSLEY
A Handbook of Marks on Pottery and Porcelain
Chaffers
NELLIE'S PROMISE
SUZEL'S ESCAPE
FOUR HUNDRED ANIMAL STORIES
A DESERT SCOUT
THE HAND ON THE BRIDLE
K.M. MACLEOD
PICKERING & INGLIS
THE LION
BLACK
Scouts and Comrades
OPENING A CHESTNUT BURR
BY E.P. ROE
OF DISTINGUISHED ANIMALS
H. PERRY ROBINSON
COUNT UP THE SUNNY DAYS
SPCK

Opposite and this page: With bookstores in every nook and cranny, Hay-on-Wye has well earned its moniker, "The Town of Books." Above: The Honesty Bookshop at Hay Castle collects revenue based on the honor system.

Tea & Tranquility

Amid the mingling scents of old books and freshly baked scones, teatime at The Signet Library offers a tantalizing opportunity to find repose during a visit to Scotland's bustling capital city.

SIGNET
LIBRARY

The Royal Mile serves as Edinburgh's main throughfare, where the Edinburgh Castle perches atop Castle Rock at one end and the Palace of Holyroodhouse anchors the other. Tucked within the myriad bustling businesses situated in between lies Colonnades at the Signet Library, a quiet oasis where the cacophony of city life fades away and the taking of tea is a cherished ritual.

Served within the surroundings of the beautifully restored Lower Library, afternoon tea surpasses simple sustenance to become a sublime experience. Fluted Corinthian columns encircling the seating area rise to an upper gallery with neoclassical-style balustrades, all wearing crowns of gold, while sunlight filters through the windows, embracing the salon in a sense of calm. This halcyon setting is just a preview of the excellent offerings to come.

From the amuse-bouche at the beginning to the three tiers of sweetness at the end, and every wonderful delight in between, the menu brims with creativity and culinary perfection. Since the chefs insist on using only the freshest and highest-quality ingredients, they love to lean into the seasons for flavor inspiration and unique combinations, such as Winter Vegetable Pithivier, Chicken Balmoral Pie, and Masala Chai Panna Cotta. No matter the day or the season, a visit to Colonnades at the Signet Library will leave a lasting impression—and prompt a promise to return.

POMMERY

The Signet Library is home to The Society of Writers to His Majesty's Signet, which dates to the fifteenth century. The building itself was completed in 1822, and a meticulous restoration returned the structure to its former glory. With vintage volumes related to the law filling bookshelves, the working library offers a splendid atmosphere for sipping and savoring among the stacks. Clockwise from below left: Custom-made three-tiered silver tea stands showcase the tearoom's scrumptious offerings, which range from traditional sweets and savories to unexpected flavor pairings that quickly become patrons' new favorites. The salon serves a wonderful array of fine teas, including the exclusive Signet Blend, a mix of Assam and Ceylon.

Remembering JANE AUSTEN

Lauded for her social commentary on the British landed gentry, the principal writer of classic Regency fiction remains one of the most beloved novelists of all time. Trailing her steps, whether to stroll through the English countryside or to dance in the city, introduces admirers to sites where the author picked up her pen and left an indelible mark on literature.

The Jane Austen Festival features a promenade of readers—all attired in Regency finery—making their way through Bath, a city mentioned in all her novels and a stunning backdrop for honoring the author's legacy.

Following the paths Jane Austen traveled at the turn of the nineteenth century leads thousands of ardent fans to England to explore the contrasting worlds she once inhabited. Amid the grand Georgian architecture of Bath—a sophisticated town that was the hub of society in her day—a permanent exhibition and an annual gathering commemorate the notable figure. Approximately eighty miles away, the village of Chawton, where she resided during her final years, brings to light an intimate portrait and offers glimpses of a quiet life.

Renowned primarily for six of her novels, including *Pride and Prejudice* and *Emma*, Austen garnered critical acclaim with the release of her first anonymously published book, *Sense and Sensibility*. Her identity was revealed posthumously, and her literary star continued to rise.

"OH, WHO CAN EVER BE TIRED OF BATH?" —Jane Austen

The Jane Austen Centre in Bath occupies a historic town house on Gay Street, a setting referenced in *Persuasion*. The authoress likely traversed this thoroughfare often, as she visited the metropolis twice before moving there with her parents and her sister, Cassandra, in 1801. Displays at this period property demonstrate the city's influence on Austen's writing. The on-site tearoom affords such culinary pleasures as Tea with Mr. Darcy, a meal featuring a scone with Dorset clotted cream and seasonal jam, assorted finger sandwiches, and homemade cakes.

A worthy excursion, Jane Austen's House Museum in Chawton welcomes guests to the cottage where she settled with her mother and Cassandra in 1809. In this haven, Austen experienced the greatest productivity of her career. Today, antique furnishings, original manuscripts, and personal effects serve as the novelist's memoir.

The ten-day Jane Austen Festival, held in September, draws throngs to Bath for more than seventy events, from readings and tours to concerts. The celebration opens with a costumed parade and culminates in a Regency-style ball.

Danish scholar Maria Rathje, who studied English at the University of Copenhagen and has lent her talents to the gala, cites contemporary heroines and clever use of satire as attributes that render the author's plots timeless. "Her lively characters subtly expose the folly of humans in ways that we can still recognize," Maria says. "I believe that most modern women would aspire to be like Elizabeth Bennet." Whether fascination lies with a favorite protagonist or with Austen herself, visiting locales where her stories unfolded allows readers the perfect opportunity to walk in her shoes.

"LET OTHER PENS DWELL ON GUILT AND MISERY. I QUIT SUCH ODIOUS SUBJECTS AS SOON AS I CAN."

—Jane Austen

Popular during the time of Jane Austen, Savoy Cake is well-suited to baking in a moulded pan. Fresh berries, edible blooms, and piped decorations of royal icing complete the festive dessert.

Savoy Cake

Makes 1 (10-cup) Bundt cake

Clarified butter, for greasing
Granulated sugar, for dusting
½ cup **all-purpose flour**
½ cup **cornstarch**
½ teaspoon **baking powder**
6 large **eggs**, room temperature and separated
¾ cup **granulated sugar**, divided
1 teaspoon **vanilla bean paste**
1 tablespoon **lemon zest**
¼ teaspoon **kosher salt**
¼ teaspoon **cream of tartar**
Royal Icing (recipe follows)
Garnish: fresh **fruit**

1. Preheat oven to 350°.
2. Brush a 10-cup Bundt pan* with clarified butter, careful to coat crevices. Dust with sugar, rotating pan to ensure an even coating and discarding any excess. Refrigerate pan until ready to use.
3. In a medium bowl, whisk together flour, cornstarch, and baking powder.
4. In the bowl of a stand mixer fitted with the whisk attachment, combine egg yolks and ½ cup sugar. Beat at medium-high speed until yolks are pale, thick, and a ribbon-like consistency, 3 to 5 minutes. With mixer at low speed, gradually add flour mixture. Beat at low speed until combined. Beat in vanilla bean paste, lemon zest, and salt. Spoon into a large bowl.
5. Clean bowl of stand mixer and whisk attachment. Using the whisk attachment, beat egg whites and cream of tartar at medium-high speed until soft peaks form, about 2 minutes. Gradually add remaining ¼ cup sugar in a slow, steady stream, beating until combined. Increase mixer speed to high, and beat until medium-soft peaks form, about 2 minutes. Add egg whites into egg yolk mixture in three additions, folding with a rubber spatula until just combined. Spoon batter into prepared pan, gently smoothing as needed.
6. Bake until cake is puffed and a wooden pick inserted near center comes out clean, about 35 minutes. Let cake rest in pan for 5 minutes, then turn out onto a wire rack covered in parchment paper to let cool completely.
7. Move cake to a serving plate. Spoon Royal Icing into a piping bag fitted with a small round tip. Pipe Royal Icing onto cake and garnish with fresh fruit as desired.

**We used the Nordic Ware Chiffon Bundt Pan.*

Royal Icing

Makes approximately 1½ cups

1¾ cups **confectioners' sugar**
1 tablespoon **meringue powder**
3 tablespoons warm **water** (105° to 110°)
½ teaspoon **vanilla extract**
1 to 2 tablespoons **water**

1. In the bowl of a stand mixer fitted with the paddle attachment, beat confectioners' sugar and meringue powder at low speed until combined. Slowly add 3 tablespoons warm water and vanilla extract, beating until fluid, about 1 minute. Increase mixer speed to medium, and beat until stiff, 4 to 5 minutes. Add water, 1 tablespoon at a time, until icing reaches desired consistency (see Note).
2. Transfer icing to a large shallow bowl; cover with a damp paper towel until ready to use. Using a wooden pick, pop and fill as many air bubbles that rise to the surface as possible before using. Store in an airtight container for up to 3 days.

Note: Icing needs to be a stiff consistency to adhere to cake without dripping.

SEASONAL BLENDS

As the earth makes its slow orb around the sun, one of the most exhilarating rituals is that of selecting special blends and tempting offerings that pair well with nature's prevailing song. Recommended reading selections to accompany the sacred cycle lend extra delight to the year's unfolding.

Winter's WARMING CUP

Set a fireside table on a chilly afternoon with good friends, small bites, and a steaming pot of tea. Graciously unconditional, this loyal tonic for the soul gives us hope, solace, and an open invitation to live in the moment.

Above left: A plate of distinctively shaped sandwiches creates a hearty mix of options to satisfy late-afternoon appetites. Wrapped in thin strips of English cucumber, rectangular Roast Beef Finger Sandwiches are layered with provolone cheese and Horseradish Cream. Egg slices and fresh dill garnish triangular Egg-and-Olive Salad Tea Sandwiches, while sprigs of oregano highlight rounds of the signature ingredient in Smoked Salmon Tea Sandwiches.

Accompany this menu with a variety of gentle tea flavors that will enhance the delicate tastes and textures. Choose from among your local specialty market's assortment of soothing oolongs, herbal infusions, or green and white varieties to complement both sweet and savory offerings.

Above left: Served with jam and clotted cream, our Cream Cheese Scones bake up golden brown. These teatime favorites are delightfully balanced with the perfect amount of sugar and then lightly coated with cream before baking for a melt-in-your-mouth finish.

Below left: Indulge sugar cravings with a selection of miniature desserts, Inspire thoughts of springtime with sublime confections, including, shown clockwise from top right, Opera Cake dressed in luscious cream cheese mousse and White Chocolate Ganache Tartlets crowned with edible flowers. For a final tasty flourish, bite-size Éclairs with Vanilla Pastry Cream are dipped in and decorated with melted candy coatings.

RECIPES

Smoked Salmon Tea Sandwiches

Makes 8

½ cup **mayonnaise**
¼ cup **sour cream**
2 tablespoons chopped fresh **dill**
8 slices **white bread**
2 (3-ounce) packages **smoked salmon**
8 slices **pancetta**, cooked
Garnish: fresh **oregano**

1. In a small bowl, combine mayonnaise and sour cream. Add dill, stirring to combine; set aside.
2. Using a 2-inch round cutter, cut 2 rounds from each bread slice. Using same cutter, cut 8 rounds from salmon.
3. Spread approximately ½ teaspoon mayonnaise mixture onto each of 8 bread rounds. Top each with 1 slice pancetta, another bread round, and salmon. Garnish with oregano, if desired.

Egg-and-Olive Salad Tea Sandwiches

Makes 16

16 slices **pumpernickel bread**
5 hard-cooked **eggs**, peeled and divided
¾ cup finely chopped **green olives**
2 tablespoons **mayonnaise**
1 tablespoon **whole-grain mustard**
1 tablespoon chopped fresh **dill**
Garnish: fresh **dill sprigs**

1. Cut bread into 3½-inch squares, removing crusts and discarding scraps.
2. Finely chop 4 eggs.
3. In a small bowl, combine eggs, olives, mayonnaise, mustard, and dill.
4. Divide mixture among 8 bread squares; top with remaining 8 bread squares. Cut each sandwich in half diagonally. Top with remaining 1 egg, sliced, and dill sprigs.

Roast Beef Finger Sandwiches with Horseradish Cream

Makes 8 sandwiches

8 slices **wheat bread**
Horseradish Cream (recipe follows)
4 slices **provolone cheese**
¼ pound thin deli-sliced **roast beef**
1 **English cucumber**, peeled into thin strips

1. Trim crusts from bread slices. Spread 4 bread slices with Horseradish Cream. Layer each with a slice of cheese. Divide roast beef among bread slices. Top with remaining 4 bread slices.
2. Cut each sandwich into 2 (3x1½-inch) fingers. Wrap each sandwich finger with a cucumber peel.

Horseradish Cream

Makes 1 cup

1 (3-ounce) package **cream cheese**, softened
½ cup **sour cream**
2 tablespoons fresh grated **horseradish**
1 teaspoon **Worcestershire sauce**
½ teaspoon **kosher salt**
½ teaspoon ground **black pepper**

In a small bowl, beat cream cheese and sour cream with a mixer at medium speed until smooth. Add horseradish, Worcestershire sauce, salt, and pepper, stirring to combine. Refrigerate in an airtight container for up to 3 days.

Cream Cheese Scones

Makes approximately 12

2 cups **all-purpose flour**
1 tablespoon **baking powder**
3 tablespoons **granulated sugar**
½ teaspoon **salt**
¼ cup chilled **unsalted butter**, diced
¼ cup chilled **cream cheese**, diced
1 cup plus 3 tablespoons **heavy whipping cream**, divided

1. Preheat oven to 350°. Line a baking sheet with parchment paper.
2. In a medium bowl, combine flour, baking powder, sugar, and salt. Using a pastry blender, cut in butter and cream cheese until mixture resembles coarse crumbs. Add 1 cup cream to flour mixture, stirring until a moist dough forms.
3. On a lightly floured surface, roll dough to a ½- to ¾-inch thickness. Using a 3-inch round cutter, cut scones, rerolling scraps no more than twice.
4. Place scones 2 inches apart on prepared pan. Using a pastry brush, lightly coat scones with remaining 3 tablespoons cream.
5. Bake until golden brown, about 15 minutes. Let cool on pan for 5 minutes. Serve warm or transfer to a wire rack to let cool completely.

White Chocolate Ganache Tartlets

Makes 24

3 (4-ounce) bars **white chocolate**, chopped
¼ cup plus 3 tablespoons **heavy whipping cream**
¼ cup **butter**

COZY SELECTIONS FOR WINTER READING

For warm hearthside moments certain to counter the bracing chill of the coldest months of the year, snuggle close to the fire with these classics recommended by the editors of *Victoria*.

- *A Christmas Carol* by Charles Dickens
- *A Little Princess* by Frances Hodgson Burnett
- *Heidi* by Johanna Spyri
- *Jane Eyre* by Charlotte Brontë
- *Little Women* by Louisa May Alcott
- *Stopping by Woods on a Snowy Evening* by Robert Frost
- *The Hobbit* by J. R. R. Tolkien
- *The Lion, the Witch and the Wardrobe* by C. S. Lewis
- *The Long Winter* by Laura Ingalls Wilder
- *To Kill a Mockingbird* by Harper Lee
- *Wuthering Heights* by Emily Brontë

2 tablespoons **light corn syrup**
1 (6.3-ounce) box **miniature tartlet shells***
Garnish: **edible flowers**

1. In a medium bowl, place chocolate.
2. In a medium saucepan, bring cream, butter, and syrup to a boil over high heat. Pour hot cream mixture over chocolate; whisk until smooth. Spoon approximately ½ teaspoon chocolate mixture into each tartlet shell.
3. Refrigerate until set, about 2 hours. Garnish with edible flowers, if desired.

**We used Clearbrook Farms Mini Bite-Size Sweet Tart Shells.*

Opera Cake
Makes 36 cake bites

1½ (8-ounce) packages **cream cheese**, softened
¾ cup **confectioners' sugar**
1 teaspoon **almond extract**
2 cups **heavy whipping cream**
1 recipe **Vanilla Pound Cakes** (recipe follows)
1½ cups prepared **apricot preserves**

1. In a large bowl, beat cream cheese with a mixer at medium speed until creamy, about 5 minutes. Add confectioners' sugar and almond extract; beat until combined.
2. In a separate large bowl, beat cream at medium-high speed until stiff peaks form. Add cream to cream cheese mixture and beat until combined.
3. Using a serrated knife, remove crusts from Vanilla Pound Cakes, and slice each cake lengthwise into 3 equal layers, leveling tops, if necessary.
4. Spread an even glaze of apricot preserves onto each cake layer, dividing preserves equally. Spread approximately ¾ cup cream cheese mousse onto 2 layers of cake and stack. Repeat with remaining cake layers and mousse. Spoon remaining 2 cups mousse into a pastry bag fitted with a small round tip. Pipe mousse in lines along length of tops of cakes. Freeze for approximately 1 hour. Using an electric knife, cut cakes into 12 equal portions.

Vanilla Pound Cakes
Makes 2 (10x5-inch) cakes

1 cup **butter**, softened
2½ cups **granulated sugar**
5 large **eggs**
3¼ cups **cake flour**, sifted
¼ teaspoon **baking soda**
1 cup **vanilla yogurt**
2 tablespoons **heavy whipping cream**
2 teaspoons **vanilla extract**

1. Preheat oven to 300°. Spray 2 (10x5-inch) loaf pans with baking spray. Line bottoms of pans with parchment paper; spray again and set aside.
2. In a large bowl, beat butter with a mixer at high speed for 1 minute. Add sugar and beat until creamy, 3 minutes. Reduce mixer speed to medium. Add eggs, one at a time, beating well after each addition, and scraping down sides of bowl as necessary.
3. In a separate large bowl, sift together flour and baking soda.
4. In a small bowl, combine yogurt, cream, and vanilla extract.
5. Add yogurt mixture to butter mixture, beating to combine. Reduce mixer speed to low.
6. Add flour mixture to butter mixture in 3 batches, beating well after each addition.
7. Divide batter between prepared pans. Bake for 1 hour, or until a wooden pick inserted near centers comes out clean. Let cool in pans for 15 minutes; remove to wire racks to cool completely.

Éclairs with Vanilla Pastry Cream

Makes approximately 36 éclairs

1 cup plus 1 tablespoon **water**, divided
½ cup **butter**, diced
1 cup **all-purpose flour**
¼ teaspoon **salt**
4 large **eggs**
Vanilla Pastry Cream (recipe follows)
½ (16-ounce) package **chocolate-flavored candy coating**, melted
½ (16-ounce) package **vanilla-flavored candy coating**, melted

1. Preheat oven to 400°. Line a baking sheet with parchment paper.
2. In a medium saucepan, bring 1 cup water and butter to a boil over medium heat. Add flour and salt; using a wooden spoon, stir vigorously until mixture forms a ball, about 3 minutes. Remove from heat and let cool for 5 minutes.
3. In the bowl of a stand mixer, beat flour mixture at high speed for 2 minutes. Add eggs, one at a time, beating well after each addition and using a spatula to scrape down sides as necessary.
4. Spoon mixture into a pastry bag fitted with a medium round tip. Pipe mixture in 3-inch logs onto prepared pan. Using remaining 1 tablespoon water to moisten your fingertip, gently smooth dough.
5. Bake until golden brown, 20 to 25 minutes. Remove from oven and let cool on pan for 10 minutes; transfer to wire racks to let cool completely.
6. Using a knife, pierce the top of each éclair, leaving a ¼-inch hole. Spoon Vanilla Pastry Cream into a pastry bag fitted with a ¼-inch tip and pipe into éclairs. Dip bottom side of each éclair into melted candy coating. Place dipped side up on parchment paper to let set.
7. Drizzle with alternating flavors of melted candy coating. Refrigerate in an airtight container for up to 3 days or freeze for up to 6 weeks.

Vanilla Pastry Cream

Makes approximately 1¼ cups

1 cup **milk**
½ teaspoon **vanilla extract**
½ **vanilla bean**, split lengthwise, seeds scraped and reserved
½ cup **granulated sugar**, divided
¼ teaspoon **salt**
2 large **egg yolks**
2 tablespoons **cornstarch**
2 tablespoons **butter**, softened

1. In a small saucepan, bring milk, vanilla extract, reserved vanilla bean seeds, ¼ cup sugar, and salt to a boil over medium heat; reduce heat and simmer for 5 minutes. Remove from heat.
2. In a medium bowl, combine egg yolks, cornstarch, and remaining ¼ cup sugar; whisk until smooth. Gradually add milk mixture to egg mixture and whisk until combined.
3. Return mixture to saucepan. Cook over medium heat, whisking constantly, until mixture boils. Remove from heat and add butter, whisking until melted. Strain mixture through a fine-mesh sieve into a bowl; cover surface of pastry cream with plastic film.
4. Chill for at least 2 hours before using. Refrigerate in an airtight container for up to 3 days.

A Springtime Ode to *The Enchanted April*

This charming tale by Elizabeth von Arnim follows four female characters—strangers drawn by an ad for a retreat at a castle on the shores of the Mediterranean. Escaping London for a joint holiday in Italy, the women develop new friendships that are remembered here with afternoon tea.

When Mrs. Wilkins, Mrs. Arbuthnot, Mrs. Fisher, and Lady Caroline venture to an ancient villa in The Enchanted April, *the four often come together at teatime. Chefs in our test kitchens enrich the story with a vibrant menu.*

Opposite: Panettone Scones offer a fitting introduction to the repast, alongside Chilled English Pea Soup. This page, clockwise from above left: Bringing a taste of Rome are Bruschetta Canapés, savory triangles topped with a seasoned Campari tomato mixture. Before broaching the subject of taking a sojourn without her husband, Mrs. Wilkins prepares a special meal for him. Her main course finds its way to our table in Beef and Herb Yorkshire Puddings. Our Macaroons might even surpass the delicious coconut drop cookies sampled by Lady Caroline at San Salvatore—"the best and biggest she had ever come across." Just as the characters in this tale find themselves transformed by their time together, may all who gather for tea experience a similar sense of renewal.

CHARMING IDEAS FOR SPRING READING

As flowers unfurl their petals, answer the call of nature by gathering for an alfresco afternoon tea themed to *The Enchanted April* by Elizabeth von Arnim or one of our other seasonal suggestions.

- *Alice's Adventures in Wonderland* by Lewis Carroll
- *All Creatures Great and Small* by James Herriot
- *Anne of Green Gables* by L. M. Montgomery
- *Emma* by Jane Austen
- *The Great Gatsby* by F. Scott Fitzgerald
- *Lilac Girls* by Martha Hall Kelly
- *Middlemarch* by George Eliot
- *The Secret Garden* by Frances Hodgson Burnett
- *The Tale of Peter Rabbit* by Beatrix Potter
- *The Wind in the Willows* by Kenneth Grahame

RECIPES

Panettone Scones

Makes 8

2 cups **all-purpose flour**
¼ cup **granulated sugar**
2 teaspoons **baking powder**
2 teaspoons **lemon zest**
½ teaspoon **kosher salt**
¼ teaspoon ground **anise seed**
¼ cup cold **unsalted butter**, cubed
½ cup chopped **pine nuts**, toasted
½ cup **raisins**
¼ teaspoon **vanilla extract**
¾ cup cold **heavy whipping cream**
1 large **egg**
1 tablespoon **water**
1 tablespoon **pearl sugar**
Mascarpone, for serving
Fruit preserves, for serving

1. Line a rimmed baking sheet with parchment paper.
2. In a large bowl, whisk together flour, granulated sugar, baking powder, lemon zest, salt, and anise. Using a pastry blender or 2 forks, cut in cold butter until mixture resembles coarse crumbs. Add pine nuts and raisins, stirring to combine. Add vanilla extract and cold cream, stirring with a fork just until dry ingredients are moistened. Working gently, bring mixture together with hands until a dough forms.
3. Turn out dough onto a lightly floured surface, and gently knead until smooth, 4 to 5 times. On a very lightly floured surface, pat dough to a 7-inch smooth disk (approximately 1-inch thick). Using a bench scraper or a thin-bladed knife dipped in flour, cut disk into 8 wedges. Place on prepared pan approximately 1½ inches apart. Freeze until firm, about 15 minutes.
4. Preheat oven to 375°.
5. In a small bowl, whisk together egg and 1 tablespoon water. Brush scones with egg wash. Sprinkle with pearl sugar.
6. Bake until golden brown and a wooden pick inserted into centers comes out clean, 20 to 25 minutes. Let cool on pan for 5 minutes. Serve warm with mascarpone and fruit preserves, if desired.

Chilled English Pea Soup

Makes 4 cups

1 (12-ounce) bag frozen shelled **peas**, thawed
1 cup roughly chopped **brioche** (see Note)
2 cups **vegetable stock**
2 tablespoons chopped fresh **chives**
½ cup fresh **parsley**
1 teaspoon **kosher salt**
⅓ cup **extra-virgin olive oil**
Goat Cheese Cream (recipe follows)
Shiitake Mushroom Bacon (recipe follows)
Garnish: fresh **chives**, fresh **parsley**, fresh **radish micro greens**

1. In the container of a blender, add peas, bread, stock, chives, parsley, and salt; blend on high speed until smooth, about 2 minutes.
2. With blender running, add olive oil in a slow and steady stream until incorporated and soup is smooth. Refrigerate to chill.
3. To serve, divide mixture among soup bowls. Drizzle with Goat Cheese Cream and sprinkle with Shiitake Mushroom Bacon. Garnish with chives, parsley, and micro greens, if desired.

Note: Remove and discard crusts from bread before chopping. Alternatively, use scraps from Bruschetta Canapés.

Goat Cheese Cream

Makes approximately ⅔ cup

3 tablespoons **goat cheese**
½ cup **heavy whipping cream**
¼ teaspoon **kosher salt**

In a small bowl, whisk together goat cheese, cream, and salt.

Shiitake Mushroom Bacon

Makes approximately ½ cup

1 (3.5-ounce) package **shiitake mushrooms**, stems removed, thinly sliced
1 tablespoon **dark sesame oil**
1 tablespoon **olive oil**
1 teaspoon **kosher salt**

1. Preheat oven to 350°. Line a baking sheet with parchment paper.
2. In a medium bowl, toss mushrooms with sesame oil, olive oil, and salt until well coated. Spread mushrooms in an even layer on prepared pan.
3. Bake until golden brown and crispy, 20 to 23 minutes, checking after 10 minutes. Let cool completely.

Beef and Herb Yorkshire Puddings

Makes 12

1 (½-pound) **beef tenderloin**, trimmed
2 teaspoons **kosher salt**, divided
1 teaspoon freshly ground **black pepper**
1 tablespoon **canola oil**
3 tablespoons **unsalted butter**
1 clove **garlic**, mashed
1 sprig fresh **thyme**
1 teaspoon fresh **rosemary**, chopped
1½ cups **whole milk**, room temperature

3 large **eggs**, room temperature
¼ cup plus 4 teaspoons **unsalted butter**, melted and divided
1½ cups **all-purpose flour**
Herb Cream (recipe follows)
Garnish: fresh **thyme**

1. Preheat oven to 375°.
2. Let tenderloin stand at room temperature for 30 minutes.
3. Season tenderloin with 1 teaspoon salt and pepper on all sides.
4. In an 8-inch cast-iron skillet, heat oil over medium-high heat. Add tenderloin to pan; let sear until a crust forms, 1½ to 2 minutes per side, reducing heat to medium if necessary. Add butter, garlic, thyme, and rosemary. Once butter has melted, baste tenderloin for 1 to 2 minutes.
5. Place skillet in oven and cook until an instant-read thermometer inserted in thickest portion registers 140°, 7 to 9 minutes, or to desired doneness.
6. Remove from skillet and let rest on a cutting board for 5 to 10 minutes; cover with foil. Slice tenderloin into 12 (¼-inch) thick slices; cut each slice into 3 pieces. Set aside to let cool to room temperature.
7. Increase oven to 425°.
8. In the container of a blender, place milk, eggs, 4 teaspoons melted butter, flour, and remaining 1 teaspoon salt. Blend on low until smooth, about 30 seconds. Let rest for 10 minutes.
9. Place a 12-cup muffin tin in oven for 5 minutes to preheat. Carefully remove from oven, and quickly pour remaining ¼ cup melted butter into 12 muffin cups (1 teaspoon each).
10. Return pan to oven for 2 minutes. Carefully remove from oven. Working quickly, pour batter into muffin cups, dividing evenly among each, approximately ¼ cup each.
11. Bake until puffed and golden brown, 15 to 20 minutes. Run a knife around edges of cups and remove puddings.
12. Top puddings with Herb Cream and 3 slices tenderloin. Garnish with thyme, if desired. Serve warm.

Herb Cream

Makes approximately ½ cup

½ cup **crème fraîche**
1 tablespoon prepared **horseradish**
1 tablespoon chopped fresh **rosemary**
2 teaspoons chopped fresh **thyme**
1 teaspoon fresh ground **black pepper**
1 teaspoon **kosher salt**

In a small bowl, combine crème fraîche, horseradish, rosemary, thyme, pepper, and salt until fully combined. Cover and refrigerate until ready to use.

Bruschetta Canapés

Makes 12

4 to 5 slices **brioche**, crusts removed, cut into 12 (2½-inch) triangles
½ cup seeded and diced **Campari tomato**
¼ cup marinated **artichokes**, drained, finely chopped
1 tablespoon **extra-virgin olive oil**
2 teaspoons **red wine vinegar**
1½ teaspoons chopped fresh **basil**
1 teaspoon minced **shallot**
1 teaspoon chopped fresh **parsley**
½ teaspoon chopped fresh **oregano**
½ teaspoon **kosher salt**
¼ teaspoon ground **black pepper**
1 clove **garlic**, finely minced
Garnish: chopped fresh **oregano**

1. Preheat oven to 325°. Line a baking sheet with parchment paper.
2. Place bread on prepared pan. Bake until golden brown and crisp completely through, 10 to 15 minutes.
3. In a medium bowl, combine tomatoes, artichokes, olive oil, vinegar, basil, shallot, parsley, oregano, salt, pepper, and garlic. Stir to combine.
4. Place approximately 1 teaspoon tomato mixture on each crostino. Garnish with oregano, if desired. Serve immediately.

Macaroons

Makes 15

4 **egg whites**, room temperature
½ cup **granulated sugar**
1 tablespoon packed **orange zest**
½ teaspoon **vanilla extract**
¼ teaspoon **kosher salt**
1 (14-ounce) bag **sweetened flaked coconut**
4 ounces **bittersweet chocolate baking bar**, finely chopped

1. Preheat oven to 300°. Line a rimmed baking sheet with parchment paper.
2. In a large bowl, whisk egg whites until foamy, about 1 minute. Whisking continuously, gradually add sugar, 1 tablespoon at a time, until well combined. Whisk in orange zest, vanilla extract, and salt. Fold in coconut. Let sit for 5 minutes.
3. Using a 2 tablespoon spring-loaded scoop, scoop coconut mixture, pack down, and level. Place at least 1½ inches apart on prepared pan.
4. Bake until edges are lightly browned, 30 to 32 minutes. Transfer pan to wire rack and let cool completely.
5. Line a separate rimmed baking sheet with parchment.
6. In a small microwave-safe bowl, microwave chocolate on high in 10-second intervals, stirring between each, until chocolate is melted and smooth (60 to 90 seconds).
7. Dip bottoms of macaroons in chocolate, letting excess drip off. Place on prepared pan. Pour remaining chocolate into a piping bag. Cut a ⅛-inch opening and drizzle over macaroons as desired. Refrigerate until chocolate is set, about 20 minutes. Using a large offset spatula, loosen macaroons from parchment, if necessary. Store in an airtight container at room temperature.

A *Summertime* AFTERNOON TEA

Gathering fresh berries offers the sweetest of rewards when the bounty finds its way into a delectable alfresco menu bursting with the succulent flavors of the season.

Under the shade of an old oak tree, dappled sunlight falls on a cheerful teatime tableau. Embroidered linens and Wedgwood Wild Strawberry china lend elegance to the relaxed setting, while handfuls of chamomile blooms hint to the delicious fare to come.

Clockwise from above left: Encapsulating favorite flavors of summer in a satisfying treat, fresh-baked Blackberry-Thyme Scones showcase a harmonious mingling of fruit and herb; a dollop of homemade lemon curd adds a refreshing burst of citrus. Progressing to the savories course makes way for our Mustard Chicken Salad Cups: crisp phyllo shells filled with the requisite Dijon-kissed mixture and topped with arugula. Cherry tomatoes, mozzarella, balsamic glaze, and basil meet atop white bread to create our refreshing Open-Faced Caprese Tea Sandwiches.

Cucumber and Smoked Salmon Bites boast a delicate garnish of feathery dill. Peeling ribbons from an English cucumber before slicing gives a decorative edge to the rounds, which are crowned with a cream cheese spread and morsels of tasty smoked fish.

Our tea party culminates with the presentation of dessert. Miniature Strawberry Pies are sure to elicit gasps of delight, and guests will be even happier to learn that they are invited to take more than one. Preparing these delectable tartlets begins with making a homemade dough that holds ruby red filling thickened with tapioca flour. The treats bake until the piecrust turns golden brown. Once cooled, the sweets reach their peak of perfection with swirls of whipped cream and a sprinkling of mint. Sample this indulgence alongside other equally precious seasonal gifts, such as unhurried hours of leisure whiled away beneath a canopy of leafy branches with book in hand.

RECIPES

Blackberry-Thyme Scones with Lemon Curd

Makes 6 scones

2 cups **all-purpose flour**
¼ cup **granulated sugar**
2 teaspoons **baking powder**
2 teaspoons **lemon zest**
1 teaspoon fresh **thyme**, finely chopped
1 teaspoon **kosher salt**
¼ cup cold **unsalted butter**, cubed
⅓ cup fresh **blackberries**
¾ cup cold **heavy whipping cream**
1 large **egg**, room temperature
1 tablespoon **water**
Lemon Curd (recipe follows)
Garnish: fresh **blackberries**, fresh **thyme**

1. Line a rimmed baking sheet with parchment paper.
2. In a large bowl, whisk together flour, sugar, baking powder, lemon zest, thyme, and salt. Using a pastry blender or 2 forks, cut in cold butter until mixture resembles coarse crumbs. Add blackberries, stirring to combine. Add cold cream, stirring just until dry ingredients are moistened. Working gently, bring mixture together with hands until a dough forms.
3. Turn out dough onto a lightly floured surface and gently knead until smooth, 4 to 5 times. Roll dough to a 7-inch (approximately ¾-inch-thick) smooth disk. Using a bench scraper or a thin-bladed knife, cut disk into 6 wedges; place wedges 2 inches apart on prepared pan. Freeze until firm, about 15 minutes.
4. Preheat oven to 375°.
5. In a small bowl, whisk egg and 1 tablespoon water; brush onto scones.
6. Bake until lightly golden and a wooden pick inserted in centers comes out clean, 20 to 25 minutes. Let cool on pan for 5 minutes. Remove from pan and let cool completely on wire racks. Serve warm with Lemon Curd; garnish with blackberries and thyme, if desired.

Lemon Curd

Makes ¾ cup

⅓ cup **granulated sugar**
¼ cup **cornstarch**
1½ teaspoons **lemon zest**
¼ cup fresh **lemon juice** (approximately 1½ lemons)
1 large **egg**, room temperature
1 large **egg yolk**, room temperature
1 tablespoon **heavy whipping cream**, room temperature
¼ cup **unsalted butter**, softened

1. In the top of a double boiler, whisk together sugar, cornstarch, lemon zest and juice, egg, egg yolk, and cream. Cook over simmering water, whisking frequently, until thickened, 10 to 15 minutes.
2. Strain mixture through a fine-mesh sieve into a bowl. Add butter, 1 tablespoon at a time, whisking until combined after each addition. Cover and refrigerate until set.

Open-Faced Caprese Tea Sandwiches

Makes 6 servings

6 slices **white bread**, frozen
1 (9-ounce) container **cherry tomatoes**
1 (8-ounce) package sliced fresh **mozzarella**
Balsamic glaze*, for topping
Extra-virgin olive oil, for topping
Flaky sea salt, for topping
Garnish: fresh **basil**, cracked **black pepper**

1. Using a 2-inch square cutter, cut out 2 pieces from each slice of bread.
2. Using a mandoline, slice tomatoes into ⅛-inch-thick slices. Using a 1-inch round cutter, cut 2 circles from each slice of mozzarella. Slice each 1-inch circle in half to make 2 (⅛-inch thick) circles.
3. Shingle tomatoes and mozzarella on each slice. Drizzle with balsamic glaze and extra-virgin olive oil. Sprinkle with flaky sea salt; garnish with basil and cracked pepper, if desired.

**We used Monari Federzoni.*

Mustard Chicken Salad Cups

Makes 24

1 (approximately 9-ounce) boneless, skinless **chicken breast**
2 cups **chicken broth**
3 **peppercorns**
1 teaspoon **kosher salt**
1 **bay leaf**
½ cup **mayonnaise**
2 tablespoons **Dijon mustard**
2 tablespoon **whole grain** or **stone-ground mustard**
3 tablespoons chopped **celery**
2 tablespoons chopped **dill pickle**
24 **phyllo cups**, prepared according to package instructions
Arugula

1. In a small saucepan, bring chicken, broth, peppercorns, salt, and bay leaf to a boil; cook until a meat thermometer inserted into thickest portion of chicken registers 165°, about 10 minutes. Remove chicken and discard liquid. Let stand for 5 minutes. Using 2 forks, shred chicken. Let cool completely.
2. In a medium bowl, combine mayonnaise, Dijon, and whole grain mustard. Add celery, pickle, and chicken to mayonnaise mixture; stir to combine.
3. Place 1 tablespoon chicken salad in each cup. Top with arugula.

Cucumber and Smoked Salmon Bites

Makes 6 servings

¼ cup **cream cheese**, softened
1 tablespoon chopped **capers**
1 tablespoon chopped fresh **dill**
1 teaspoon **lemon zest**
1 large **English cucumber**, cut into 12 (¼-inch) rounds
1 (4-ounce) package **cold smoked salmon**
Garnish: fresh **dill**, **lemon zest**

1. In a small bowl, combine cream cheese, capers, dill, and lemon zest; stir until smooth.
2. Top each cucumber round with 1 teaspoon cream cheese mixture. Top with smoked salmon. Garnish with dill and lemon zest, if desired.

Miniature Strawberry Pies

Makes 20

2¼ cups **all-purpose flour**
⅔ cup **confectioners' sugar**
1 cup **unsalted butter**, softened
¼ teaspoon **kosher salt**
4 cups fresh **strawberries**, quartered
⅓ cup **granulated sugar**
⅓ cup **tapioca flour**
1 teaspoon **lemon zest**
Garnish: **sweetened whipped cream**, fresh **mint leaves**

1. In the work bowl of a food processor, pulse together all-purpose flour and confectioners' sugar. Add butter and salt; pulse until mixture is crumbly.
2. Turn out dough onto a lightly floured surface and shape dough into a disk. Cover and refrigerate until firm, about 20 minutes.
3. In a large bowl, stir together strawberries, granulated sugar, tapioca flour, and lemon zest. Let stand for 10 minutes.
4. Preheat oven to 350°. Spray 20 (2½-inch) mini tart pans with baking spray with flour. Line a rimmed baking sheet with parchment paper.
5. On a lightly floured surface, roll dough to a ⅛-inch thickness. Using a 3¾-inch round cutter, cut dough and gently press into the bottoms and up sides of prepared tart pans. Using a small rolling pin, roll over tops of tartlet pans to trim excess dough. Scoop one heaping tablespoon of strawberry mixture into each prepared tart pan. Place tart pans on prepared baking sheet.
6. Bake until edges of crusts are golden brown and filling begins to bubble, 40 to 45 minutes. Transfer to a wire rack, and let cool completely before removing tarts from pans. Garnish with whipped cream and mint leaves, if desired.

EASEFUL DAYS OF SUMMER READING

When golden sunlight stretches as far as the eye can see, fill these languid hours with fresh strawberries and cream, a pot of tea, and our must-read volumes.

- *A Midsummer Night's Dream* by William Shakespeare
- *Anne of the Island* by L. M. Montgomery
- *At Home in Mitford* by Jan Karon
- *Cranford* by Elizabeth Gaskell
- *Dandelion Wine* by Ray Bradbury
- *Gift from the Sea* by Anne Morrow Lindbergh
- *Rose in Bloom* by Louisa May Alcott
- *Sense and Sensibility* by Jane Austen
- *The Diary of a Young Girl* by Anne Frank
- *The Guernsey Literary and Potato Peel Pie Society* by Mary Ann Shaffer and Annie Barrows
- *Treasure Island* by Robert Louis Stevenson

AUTUMN GRATITUDE

Flavors of the classic Thanksgiving menu find a welcome reception at the tea table, where moments of quiet repose bid those gathered 'round to reflect on an abundance of gifts.

Our harvest fête begins with notes of citrus in Orange Cranberry Scones, featured on the previous spread, and continues with a trio of savories, this page. Clockwise from above left: Freshly baked mini loaves feature in Pumpkin Bread Tea Sandwiches, a medley of toppings crown Sweet Potato Bites, and cranberry sage aioli lends festive flair to hearty Turkey Finger Sandwiches.

"THE THANKFUL HEART OPENS OUR EYES TO A MULTITUDE OF BLESSINGS THAT CONTINUALLY SURROUND US."

—James E. Faust

GILDED HOURS OF AUTUMN READING

When burnished leaves begin to fall and crisp, cool air carries the scent of woodsmoke, turn the pages of a cherished tome while sipping a steaming cup of a favorite chai blend.

- *A Light in the Window* by Jan Karon
- *Anne's House of Dreams* by L. M. Montgomery
- *Christy* by Catherine Marshall
- *Great Expectations* by Charles Dickens
- *Little House in the Big Woods* by Laura Ingalls Wilder
- *The Lord of the Rings* by J. R. R. Tolkien
- *My Beloved* by Jan Karon
- *Northanger Abbey* by Jane Austen
- *Once Upon a Wardrobe* by Patti Callahan Henry
- *Pride and Prejudice* by Jane Austen
- *Rebecca* by Daphne du Maurier
- *Villette* by Charlotte Brontë

A cherished tradition of Thanksgiving is encouraging each guest to offer an expression of gratitude, and the ritual is even sweeter when the heartfelt sentiments are shared over dessert. Opposite: Perfectly suited to such an interlude are Apple Roses. Gleaming ruffles of the Pink Lady variety, which retains its rosy peel and alabaster flesh during baking, bring to mind the proverbial image of lovely words as apples of gold in settings of silver. Complementing these charming pastries are Pecan Pie Triangles, this page, above, with flaky crust, rich bourbon filling, and chopped nuts coming together in a delectable bar.

RECIPES

Orange Cranberry Scones

Makes approximately 12

3 cups **all-purpose flour**
2 tablespoons **granulated sugar**
4 teaspoons **baking powder**
½ teaspoon **salt**
½ cup cold **unsalted butter**, cubed
1 cup plus 2½ tablespoons cold **heavy whipping cream**
2 teaspoons **orange zest**
½ teaspoon **vanilla extract**
¼ cup **sweetened dried cranberries**, chopped
1 large **egg**, lightly beaten
Orange Glaze (recipe follows)
Garnish: **orange zest**

1. Preheat oven to 375°. Line a rimmed baking sheet with parchment paper.
2. In a large bowl, whisk together flour, sugar, baking powder, and salt. Using a pastry blender or 2 forks, cut in cold butter until mixture is crumbly.
3. In a small bowl, stir together cream, orange zest, and vanilla extract. Pour cream mixture into flour mixture, stirring with a fork just until dough starts to come together. Stir in cranberries. Knead by hand 3 or 4 times.
4. On a lightly floured surface, press dough to a ¾-inch-thick circle. Using a 2¼-inch round cutter dipped in flour, cut dough without twisting cutter, rerolling once. Place on prepared pan. Freeze until firm, 15 minutes.
5. Brush tops with lightly beaten egg, and bake until golden brown, 16 to 20 minutes. Let cool completely and drizzle with Orange Glaze. Garnish with orange zest, if desired.

Orange Glaze

Makes ¾ cup

1 cup **confectioners' sugar**
3 tablespoons fresh **orange juice**

In a small bowl, whisk together confectioners' sugar and orange juice. Use immediately.

Pumpkin Bread Tea Sandwiches

Makes 16

1 (8-ounce package) **cream cheese**, softened
1 tablespoon **orange zest**
½ cup chopped **walnuts**
Pumpkin Bread (recipe follows)

1. In a medium bowl, combine cream cheese, orange zest, and walnuts.
2. Using a serrated knife, slice Pumpkin Bread into 16 (¼-inch-thick) slices, reserving remaining mini loaves for other uses. Spread half of slices with cream cheese mixture, and top with remaining slices, reserving any remaining filling for other uses. Trim crusts from sandwiches and cut diagonally into triangles. Place sandwiches in an airtight container, with damp paper towels covering sandwiches, and refrigerate for up to one hour before serving.

Pumpkin Bread

Makes 4 mini loaves

3½ cups **all-purpose flour**
3 cups **granulated sugar**
1 tablespoon **baking powder**
½ teaspoon **kosher salt**
2 teaspoons **pumpkin pie spice**
1 teaspoon ground **ginger**
2½ cups **canned pumpkin**
4 large **eggs**
⅔ cup **water**
½ cup **vegetable oil**

1. Preheat oven to 350°. Spray 4 (5½-inch) mini loaf pans with baking spray with flour.
2. In a large bowl, whisk together flour, sugar, baking powder, salt, pumpkin pie spice, and ginger.
3. In a medium bowl, whisk together pumpkin, eggs, ⅔ cup water, and oil. Add pumpkin mixture to flour mixture, and stir until well combined. Divide batter among prepared pans.
4. Bake until a wooden pick inserted in centers comes out clean, 45 to 55 minutes. Let cool in pans for 10 minutes. Remove from pans and let cool completely on a wire rack.

Turkey Finger Sandwiches with Cranberry Sage Aioli

Makes 8 finger sandwiches

⅓ cup **mayonnaise**
2 tablespoons **cream cheese**, softened
1 teaspoon minced fresh **sage**
8 slices **whole wheat bread**, frozen
12 slices thin sliced deli-style **roast turkey**
½ cup prepared **whole-berry cranberry sauce**
Watercress
Garnish: fresh **sage leaves**

1. In a small bowl, combine mayonnaise, cream cheese, and minced sage.
2. Spread mayonnaise mixture over each frozen bread slice. Top half of bread slices with 3 turkey slices each, folding and trimming turkey to fit. Cover with an

even layer of cranberry sauce, and top with a few sprigs watercress. Cover with remaining bread slices.

3. Using a serrated knife and a gentle sawing motion, trim crusts from sandwiches to create a perfect square. Cut each sandwich into 2 rectangles.

4. Serve immediately or cover with damp paper towels, place in a covered container, and refrigerate for a few hours. Garnish with sage leaves, if desired.

Sweet Potato Bites

Makes approximately 16

2 medium **sweet potatoes,** uniformly shaped and approximately 2½ inches in diameter
2 teaspoons **olive oil**
½ teaspoon **fine sea salt**, divided
⅜ teaspoon ground **black pepper**, divided
¼ teaspoon ground **coriander**
16 wedges **Brie**
Orange sections
Salted pumpkin seeds
3 tablespoons chopped **dried sweetened cranberries**
Fresh **rosemary sprigs**
Honey

1. Preheat oven to 400°. Line a sheet pan with foil, and lightly grease with oil.

2. Using a sharp knife or mandoline, slice sweet potatoes into ¼-inch-thick disks. Place on prepared pan. Brush with olive oil.

3. In a small bowl, combine ¼ teaspoon salt, ¼ teaspoon pepper, and coriander. Sprinkle over sweet potatoes.

4. Bake until just fork tender, 8 to 10 minutes. Let cool completely on pan.

5. To serve, top with Brie, orange sections, pumpkin seeds, dried cranberries, rosemary, and a drizzle of honey.

Pecan Pie Triangles

Makes 24

Piecrust Dough (recipe follows)
1½ cups coarsely chopped **pecans**
½ cup firmly packed **light brown sugar**
5 tablespoons **all-purpose flour**
1 teaspoon **salt**
1½ cups **light corn syrup**
2 tablespoons **butter**, melted
3 large **eggs**
2 teaspoons **bourbon**
1 teaspoon **vanilla extract**

1. Preheat oven to 350°. Spray a 13x9-inch pan with baking spray with flour and line with parchment, letting excess extend over sides.

2. Press Piecrust Dough into bottom of prepared pan. Top with pecans.

3. In a medium bowl, combine brown sugar, flour, and salt. Whisk in corn syrup, melted butter, eggs, bourbon, and vanilla extract. Pour corn syrup mixture over pecans.

4. Bake until edges are a light golden brown and start to set, 18 to 22 minutes. Let cool completely in pan.

5. Using excess parchment as handles, remove from pan. Using a sharp knife, cut into 12 squares and cut each square diagonally. Store in an airtight container for up to 4 days.

Piecrust Dough

Makes 1 (13x9-inch) crust

2 cups **all-purpose flour**
2 tablespoons **granulated sugar**
¼ teaspoon **kosher salt**
¾ cup cold **unsalted butter**, cubed
3 tablespoons **ice-cold water**

In a medium bowl, whisk together flour, sugar, and salt. Using a pastry blender or 2 forks, cut in cold butter until mixture is crumbly. Stirring with a fork, add 3 tablespoons cold water just until dough starts to come together in large chunks but isn't fully combined. Use immediately.

Apple Roses

Makes 10

3 **Pink Lady Apples**
2 tablespoons fresh **lemon juice**
1 tablespoon **water**
½ cup plus 1 teaspoon **apricot preserves**, divided
1 (17.3-ounce) package frozen **puff pastry**, thawed (2 sheets)

1. Preheat oven to 375° and position oven rack in lower third of oven. Spray a 12-cup muffin pan with baking spray with flour.

2. Using a sharp knife, cut apples in half from top to bottom, core the two halves, and cut each half into approximately ⅛-inch-thick slices.

3. In a medium skillet, place slices and cover with lemon juice and 1 tablespoon water. Cook over medium-low heat until apples are pliable but not fully cooked.

4. In a small heatproof bowl, warm preserves in microwave for 20 seconds, stopping halfway through to stir.

5. Working with one pastry sheet at a time, use a rolling pin to roll pastry to a 12x10-inch rectangle. Cut pastry sheet into 5 (12x2-inch) strips. Repeat with remaining pastry sheet.

6. Brush pastry strips with 1 teaspoon preserves. Arrange apple slices (peel side up) along the top half of pastry strips, overlapping slices slightly. Starting with the short end, roll pastry up, jelly roll style, and place into prepared muffin cups with peels facing up.

7. Bake until puff pastry is golden brown, 18 to 20 minutes. Place a sheet of foil on the rack above pastries after 10 minutes to prevent apples from getting too dark.

8. Brush with remaining apricot preserves and serve immediately.

SUBLIME SETTINGS

For true bibliophiles, there's something deeply soul stirring about peeking into domiciles long ago inhabited by much-loved authors. Whether the writers penned their works in the snug environs of small romantic abodes or amidst sprawling countryside estates, we're certain a teacup was close at hand.

Exploring the BRONTË LEGACY

Once home to a country cleric and his children—including three daughters lauded for their incomparable creative talents—this West Yorkshire manse brims with a world-class cache of artifacts that speaks to the enduring allure of the literary life.

The village of Haworth and surrounding South Pennines hills—backdrops for the 2016 PBS Masterpiece television drama To Walk Invisible: The Lives of the Brontë Sisters*—might still be recognized by the legendary authors today.*

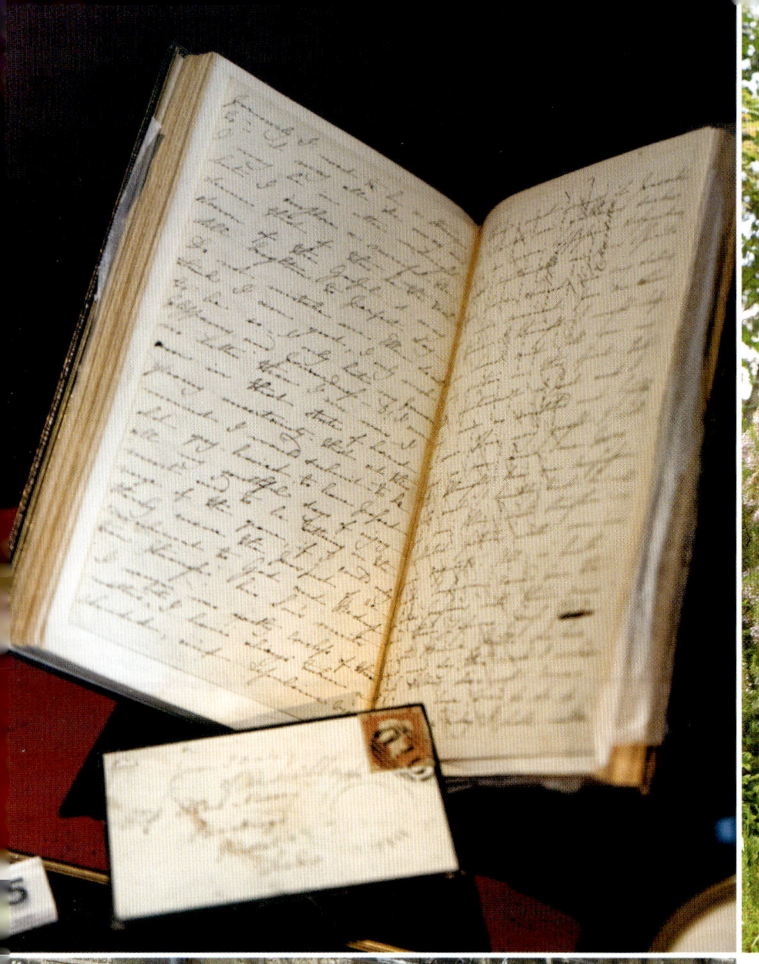

Ensconced within the moorlands of northern England, the community of Haworth, once a center for wool manufacturing, has become more widely known over the past two centuries for tales woven by enigmatic former residents. Tourists roam the village's cobblestone streets, follow ambling footpaths into the countryside, and traverse heather-covered slopes to discover settings depicted by the most famous siblings ever to pick up the pen. Area destinations, such as the Brontë Parsonage Museum, allow readers to visit sites that influenced the family's works.

Clergyman Patrick Brontë moved into Haworth Parsonage with his wife, Maria Branwell, and their children in 1820. Widowed a year later, the vicar also soon lost his two oldest daughters to illness. Under the patriarch's care, and the watchful eye of Maria's sister Elizabeth, the remaining four children—Charlotte, Branwell, Emily, and Anne—received a classic education at home. They

"YOU KNOW FULL WELL AS I DO THE VALUE OF SISTERS' AFFECTIONS: THERE IS NOTHING LIKE IT IN THIS WORLD."
—Charlotte Brontë

wrote prodigiously, growing from youngsters dreaming up adventures in imaginary realms to adults exchanging critiques.

Although Branwell, the only brother, experienced more personal struggle than professional success, the sisters achieved public acclaim. With financial support from their aunt, the trio released a collection of poetry in 1846 as Currer, Ellis, and Acton Bell, masculine pseudonyms chosen to correspond with the authoresses' initials. This effort languished commercially, selling just two copies in its original printing, but shortly after, all three debuted groundbreaking novels.

Jane Eyre was the first to launch, and the ambitious and outgoing Charlotte quickly became a celebrity in literary circles, with three additional novels to see publication.The reclusive Emily created a stir with *Wuthering Heights*, an unremitting account of star-crossed lovers, but had no desire to step from the shadows of her nom de plume to bask in its glory. The youngest sibling, Anne, considered the plight of women in *Agnes Grey* and *The Tenant of Wildfell Hall*.

Despite newfound prominence, they continued living in the parsonage, the family's haven for four decades. "My home is humble and unattractive to strangers," Charlotte once wrote, "but to me it contains what I shall find nowhere else in the world—[the] profound, and intense affection which brothers and sisters feel for each other when their minds are cast in the same mould, their ideas drawn from the same source." The abode boasts a vast treasury of "Brontëana," including manuscripts, furnishings, and keepsakes that chronicle the fascinating stories of a gifted trio who penned some of the most beloved volumes in the English language.

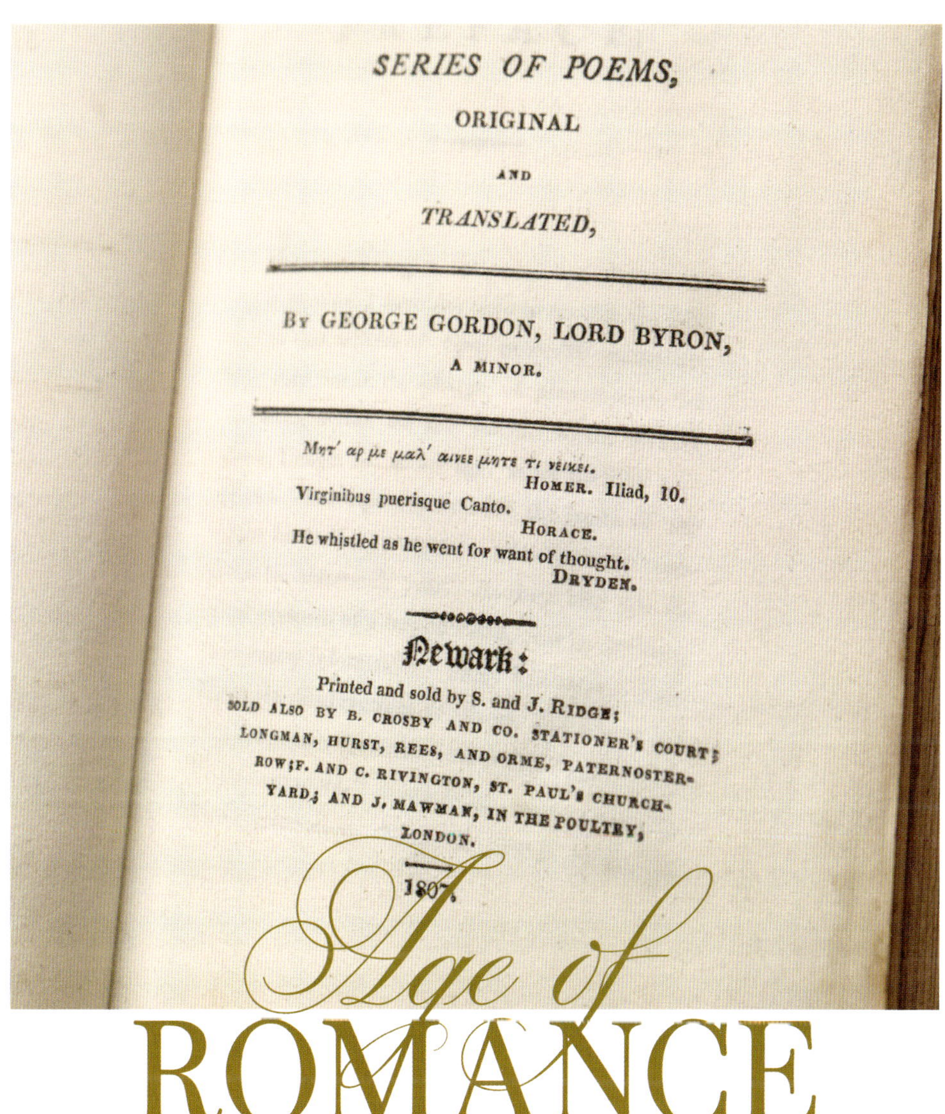

SERIES OF POEMS,

ORIGINAL

AND

TRANSLATED,

By GEORGE GORDON, LORD BYRON,

A MINOR.

Μητ' αρ με μαλ' αινεε μητε τι νεικει.
HOMER. Iliad, 10.

Virginibus puerisque Canto.
HORACE.

He whistled as he went for want of thought.
DRYDEN.

Newark:

Printed and sold by S. and J. RIDGE;
SOLD ALSO BY B. CROSBY AND CO. STATIONER'S COURT;
LONGMAN, HURST, REES, AND ORME, PATERNOSTER-ROW; F. AND C. RIVINGTON, ST. PAUL'S CHURCH-YARD; AND J. MAWMAN, IN THE POULTRY,
LONDON.

1807.

Age of ROMANCE

In the waning years of the eighteenth century, the whole tenor of British literature changed. Reason and structure gave way to emotion and imagination, ushering in the sublime movement known as Romanticism. The literary legacies of three noted scribes from this period still linger in the captivating properties that influenced their memorable compositions.

NEWSTEAD ABBEY

The River Leen flows through Nottinghamshire, England, its nourishing waters creating the verdant parkland that makes up the property known as Newstead Abbey, where George Gordon Byron, familiarly Lord Byron, lived from 1808 to 1814. Newstead, with its cavernous halls and centuries-old ruins, held great fascination for Byron. Among the many personal treasures remaining there is the desk, opposite, where he wrote much of his acclaimed verse.

Originally built as a monastery in the late twelfth century, Newstead was bequeathed to Lord Byron by his great uncle in 1798, though the writer didn't reside there until a decade later. Often considered the greatest of all the Romantic poets, the Cambridge-educated peer's travels through the Mediterranean inspired his much-touted work, long narrative poem Childe Harold's Pilgrimage. *Opposite: Comprising sixteen distinctive areas, the property's beautiful gardens are made for meandering. These singluar sanctuaries offer quiet spots to take in botanical inspiration.*

"SHE WALKS IN BEAUTY,
LIKE THE NIGHT
OF CLOUDLESS CLIMES
AND STARRY SKIES ... ."

—Lord Byron

KEATS HOUSE

It is astounding to realize that John Keats's vast catalog of work was accomplished in just a six-year span. He managed to combine medical training with poetry-writing, but, following the publication of his first book of verse in 1817, the prolific poet gave up medicine entirely. Built in 1815 and situated in London's northern neighborhood of Hampstead—a community widely known for its literary, musical, and intellectual esprit de corps—Keats House was originally known as Wentworth Place. Though it appears as one house from the outside, it was two separate residences. The wordsmith lived here as a lodger from late 1818 until 1820, penning many of his signature odes and the enigmatic ballad "La Belle Dame sans Merci."

ABBOTSFORD

After contracting polio as a toddler, Sir Walter Scott was sent to live with relatives in the Scottish countryside. As the fresh air improved his health, his kin encouraged the young boy's literary pursuits and spurred a passion for Scotland's heroic history, which greatly influenced his writing, as evidenced by works such as Ivanhoe *and* Rob Roy*. Nestled along the banks of the River Tweed in Roxburghshire, Scott's Scottish Baronial-style castle, Abbotsford, is the masterstroke of his architectural ambitions. The richly appointed yet rambling residence, which the author affectionately referred to as "a flibbertigibbet of a house" was built with the prodigious income earned from his writings. Visitors to this turreted testament to his success are privy to the personal side of the man—a keen collector whose predilections included artifacts, weaponry, and books.*

Located near his Headington home was C. S. Lewis's place of worship, Holy Trinity Church. Even before his conversion to faith, the author embodied selfless loyalty by caring for the mother and sister of his close friend, Paddy Moore, who died in World War I.

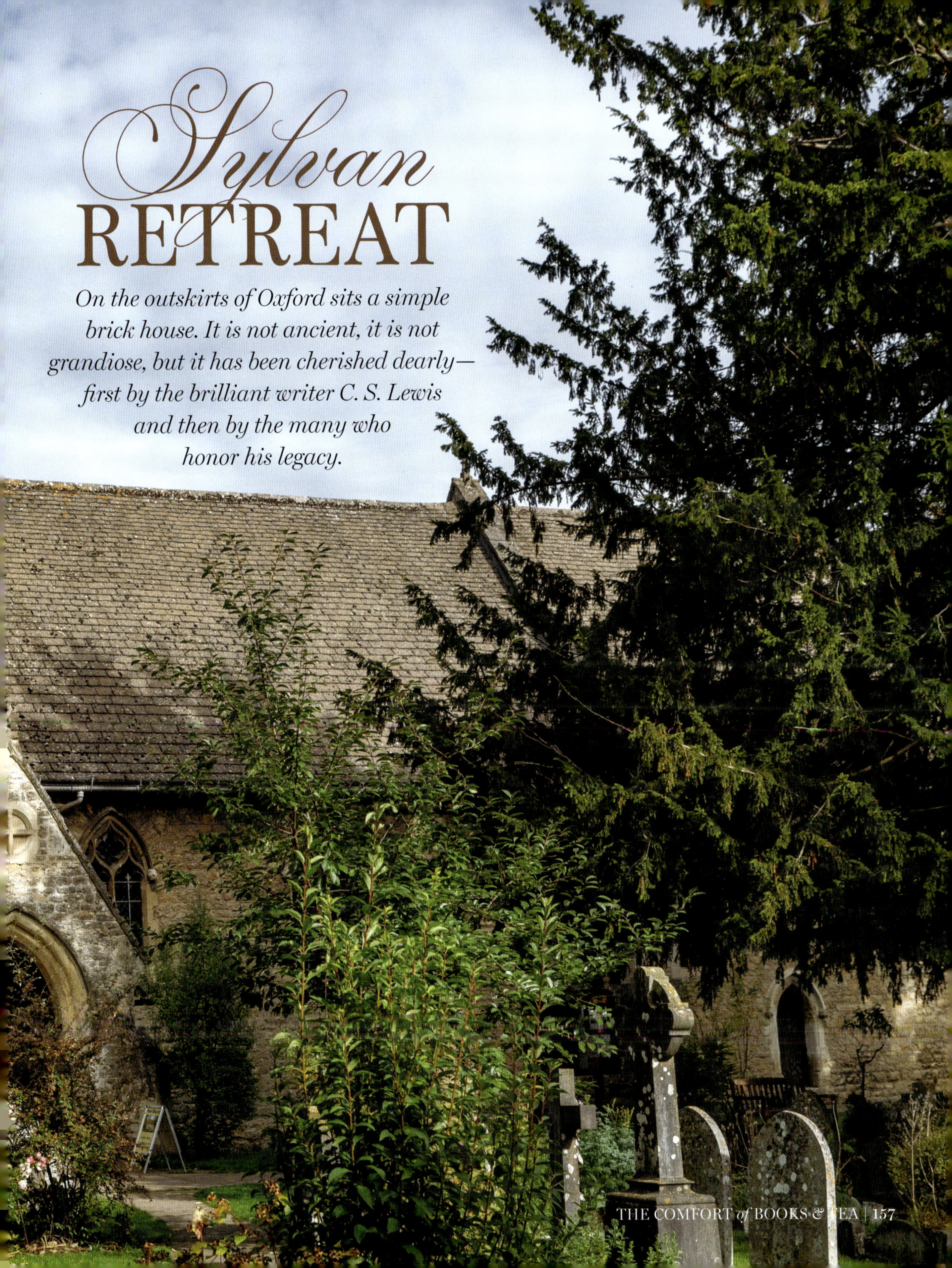

Sylvan RETREAT

On the outskirts of Oxford sits a simple brick house. It is not ancient, it is not grandiose, but it has been cherished dearly—first by the brilliant writer C. S. Lewis and then by the many who honor his legacy.

For esteemed author and apologist Clive Staples Lewis, life was not dominated by peaceful pensiveness and solitude at a desk. Though Jack, as he was known by close friends, was a true academic—earning an honorable triple first at Oxford's University College and serving as a fellow at Magdalen College before teaching at The University of Cambridge—the great mind chose to spend his later years immersed in ordinary life alongside loved ones.

The Kilns, a quaint property that began its life as a brickworks—hence the name—was Lewis's home from 1930 until his death in 1963. Located roughly an hour's walk from Oxford city center, the rural setting was "delightful" to Lewis. Its nine acres, with wooded paths and a manmade pond, may have provided a great deal of inspiration during his most creative years. While residing here with his brother, Warren; mother figure, Mrs. Moore; and eventually his wife, Joy, Lewis penned his greatest works: from intellectual reflections on English literature and faith-filled triumphs such as *Mere Christianity* to well-loved fiction stories such as the renowned *The Chronicles of Narnia*.

But the house was not the quiet retreat one might expect of a writer's residence. Friends and members of the Inklings, a literary club Lewis founded alongside J. R. R. Tolkien, would stop by for discussion. His cohabitants, although very dear to him, each struggled with various ailments prone to disturbing the peace. Still, while loyally embracing these relationships and the distractions of everyday rural Christian life, Lewis was able to pen a great number of works that continue to influence minds and souls around the world.

Today, his legacy lives on not only through his words but also at The Kilns. Though the property was divided up and sold to other owners for a time following his and brother Warnie's deaths, eventually falling into disrepair, nearly a half acre and the house have now been restored and are maintained by the C. S. Lewis Foundation. Guests may visit for guided tours of the house, which also functions as a working residence for students. This handful of individuals walk and sleep and work—and even write—in the very place that was once occupied by the beloved author himself those many years ago.

A CATHOLIC CATECHISM
WILLIAM SHAKESPEARE
OXFORD
HOWARD SPRING

Below right: The attic re-creates the Lewis brothers' childhood home in Belfast, Northern Ireland, where they read extensively and played imaginatively. Here, a wardrobe appears to open to Narnia. Opposite: This cozy den, where the author spent many pleasant hours, recalls his affinity for the enduring comforts of books and tea.

CREDITS & RESOURCES

The Comfort of Books & Tea: A Gentle Guide to Reading and Teatime
Editor: Melissa Lester
Creative Director, Lifestyle: Melissa Sturdivant Smith
Managing Editor: Leslie Bennett Smith
Senior Features Editors: Claire Henry, Lydia McMullen, Audra Shalles
Administrative Senior Art Director: Tracy Wood-Franklin
Senior Copy Editor, Lifestyle: Rhonda Lee Lother
Editorial Assistant: Elizabeth M. Scheeter
Senior Digital Imaging Specialist: Delisa McDaniel

CONTRIBUTING WRITERS
CAROL BULLMAN: page 22
KAREN CALLAWAY: pages 80–91 and 144–155
CYNTHIA REESER CONSTANTINO: pages 39–40
BRITTANY WILLIAMS FLOWERS: pages 70–73
MELISSA LESTER: pages 9, 26–33, 42–47, 54–69, 92–101, 112–135, and 138–143
OLIVIA LUZIER: pages 18–19
LYDIA MCMULLEN: pages 86–91 and 144–155
KIMBER MITCHELL: pages 34–35
CAROL RIZZOLI: pages 13–15
AUDRA SHALLES: pages 9, 25, 49, 79, 103, and 137
LESLIE BENNETT SMITH: pages 50–53 and 156–161

CONTRIBUTING PHOTOGRAPHERS
JANE HOPE: pages 79–85, 92–99, and 136–161
MAC JAMIESON: pages 17, 103, 112–117, and back cover
JOHN O'HAGAN: pages 4–5, 24, 26–31, and 50–53
KATE SEARS: pages 70–73
MARCY BLACK SIMPSON: pages 2, 12, 25, 34–41, and 104–111
STEPHANIE WELBOURNE STEELE: cover and pages 6, 8, 10, 19–20, 34, 43–44, 47–49, 54–58, 62–67, 74, 77–78, 86–91, 100, 102, 120–125, 128–133, and 154–155

CONTRIBUTING STLYISTS
MAGHAN ARMSTRONG: pages 48–49, 62–67, and 100
SIDNEY BRAGIEL: pages 4–5, 10, 24, 26–31, and 54–58
MARY LEIGH GWALTNEY: pages 104–111
YUKIE MCLEAN: pages 2, 25, and 34–41
MELISSA STURDIVANT SMITH: cover and pages 6, 8, 19–20, 34, 43–44, 47, 74, 77–78, 86–91, 102–103, 112–117, 120–125, 128–133, 154–155, and back cover

CONTRIBUTING RECIPE DEVELOPERS & FOOD STYLISTS
OLA ABODZA: pages 54–61
AARON CONRAD: pages 62–69
BECCA CUMMINS: pages 20–21, 42–47, and 112–119
KATIE MOON DICKERSON: pages 20–21, 42–47, 54–61, and 120–127
KATHLEEN KANEN: pages 26–33, 74–77, and 112–117
MEGAN LANKFORD: pages 128–135
TRICIA MANZANERO: pages 26–33
VANESSA ROCCHIO: pages 74–77, 100–101, and 128–135
AMANDA STABILE: pages 100–101
IZZIE TURNER: pages 54–69, 100–101, 112–119, and 120–127
TAYLOR FRANKLIN WANN: pages 26–33
LOREN WOOD: pages 104–111

WHERE TO VISIT & SHOP

Below is a listing of products and companies featured in this book.

Cover and pages 86–91: The Colonnades at the Signet Library, Parliament Square, Edinburgh EH1 1RF, United Kingdom, thesignetlibrary.co.uk.
Page 10: Wedgwood: Swallow (Yellow Brown Trim) Footed Demitasse Cup & Saucer; from Replacements, Ltd., replacements.com.
Pages 12–15: Carol Rizzoli is the author of several books, including *The House at Royal Oak* and the forthcoming *Desire Lines: A Memoir in 24 Moments*; carolrizzoli.org.
Page 17: Wedgwood: Oberon Teapot, Oberon Teacup, Oberon Tea Saucer; wedgwood.com.
Pages 20, 43–44, and 47: Tricia's Treasures: Antique books; triciastreasures.us.
Pages 26–31: Haviland: Cherbourg Flat Cup & Saucer Set, Cherbourg Sugar Bowl & Lid, Cherbourg Bon Bon, Cherbourg Tureen & Lid, Apple Blossom Footed Cream Soup Bowl & Saucer Set, Cherbourg Salad Plate; Noritake: Bluedawn Footed Cup & Saucer Set, Bluedawn Bread & Butter Plate; Alvin: Chateau Rose Small Solid Cold Meat Serving Fork, Chateau Rose Round Bowl Soup Spoon (Bouillon), Chateau Rose Demitasse Spoon; Mikado: MI01 Salad Plate, MI01 12" Oval Serving Platter; from Replacements, Ltd., replacements.com.

Pages 48–49 and 62–67: Juliska: Berry & Thread 16-piece Place Setting in Chambray, Sitio Stripe Dinner Plate in Delft Blue, Eyelet Napkin in Sunflower; juliska.com. Little English: Button Down Shirt in Wingate Plaid; littleenglish.com. The Village Green: Yellow Beeswax Pot, similar styles available; shopthevillagegreen.com.
Pages 50–53: Central Park Conservancy, South Garden of Central Park's Conservatory Garden, 14 East 60th Street, New York, NY, centralparknyc.org.
Pages 70–73: For more information on Beatrix Potter, visit golakes.co.uk, nationaltrust.org.uk, and yewtree-farm.com.
Pages 74 and 77: Juliska: Natural Bamboo 5-Piece Place Setting; juliska.com.
Pages 80–85: Hay on Wye Booksellers, 13–14 High Town, Hay-on-Wye, Hereford HR3 5AE, United Kingdom, hayonwyebooksellers.co.uk. The Poetry Bookshop, The Pavement, Lion Street, Hay-on-Wye, Hereford HR3 5BU, United Kingdom, poetrybookshop.co.uk. Richard Booth's Bookshop, 44 Lion Street, Hay-on-Wye, Hereford HR3 5AA, boothbooks.co.uk. Addyman Books, 39 Lion Street, Hay-on-Wye, Herefordshire, HR3 5AA, United Kingdom, hay-on-wyebooks.com. The Great English Outdoors, 19 Castle Street, Hay-on-Wye, Herefordshire HR3 5DF, greatenglish.co.uk. Goosey Ganders, Compton House, High Town, Hay-on-Wye, Hereford HR3 5AE, United Kingdom. Llewelyn & Company, 19 High Town, Hay-on-Wye, Herefordshire, HR3 5AE United Kingdom, llewelynandcompany.com. Timeless Treasures, 1 The Pavement, Hay-on-Wye, Herefordshire HR3 5BU, United Kingdom.
Pages 92–99: For more information on the Jane Austen Festival, visit janeaustens.house. Jane Austen Centre, 40 Gay Street, Bath BA1 2NT, janeausten.co.uk. Jane Austen's House Museum, Winchester Road, Chawton, Hampshire GU34 1SD, jane-austens-house-museum.org.uk.
Page 100: Corbell Silver: Oblong tray, oblong gallery tray, small oval dish, round tea set; corbellsilver.com. Royal Doulton: Sovereign Dinner Plate, English Renaissance Salad Plate, English Renaissance Footed Cup & Saucer Set, English Renaissance Rim Soup Bowl, English Renaissance Tureen & Lid; Towle Silver: King Richard flatware; from Replacements, Ltd., replacements.com.
Pages 104–111: Royal Limoges Oasis White teacup and saucer, dessert plate; Spode Stafford White teacup and saucer; antique English 5-piece tea service; Herend Gwendolyn salad plate; from Bromberg's, brombergs.com. Bernardaud Eden Turquoise teacup and saucer, bread-and-butter plate, sugar bowl, and creamer; bernardaud.com/en/us. Tiered wheat server, gold-and-white footed bowl, small round scalloped dish; from Hoover Antique Gallery, hooverantiquegalleryal.com/. Chantilly sugar tongs; from Argent Antiques.
Pages 112–117: Gabrella Manor, 8912 4th Avenue South, Birmingham, AL, gabrellamanor.com. Williams Sonoma: Palermo Sicily Oilcloth Outdoor Round Tablecloth; williams-sonoma.com. Maison de France Antiques: Chairs; mdfantiques.com. Faïencerie de Gien: Toscana Dinner Plate, Toscana Large Rim Soup Bowl, Toscana Breakfast Cup & Saucer Set, Toscana Teapot & Lid, Toscana Large Sandwich Tray, Toscana Sugar Bowl & Lid, Toscana Flat Cup & Saucer Set, Toscana Creamer, Toscana Dessert Luncheon Plate, Toscana 13" Oval Serving Platter; from Replacements, Ltd., replacements.com
Pages 120–125: Wedgwood: Wild Strawberry 146 Shape Sugar Bowl & Lid, Wild Strawberry Dinner Plate, Wild Strawberry Salad/Dessert Plate, Wild Strawberry Peony Shape Footed Cup & Saucer Set, Wild Strawberry Bread & Butter Plate, Wild Strawberry Miniature Teapot & Lid; from Replacements, Ltd., replacements.com.
Pages 128–133: Bernardaud: Sceaux Teapot & Lid, Sceaux 11" Oval Serving Platter; Haviland: Paradise Dinner Plate, Paradise Salad Plate, Paradise Sugar Bowl & Lid, Paradise Creamer Eden Flat Cup & Saucer Set, Paradise 12" Chop Plate; from Replacements, Ltd., replacements.com.
Pages 136–143: Brontë Parsonage Museum, Church Street, Haworth, West Yorkshire BD22 8DR, England, bronte.org.uk.
Pages 144–155: Newstead Abbey, Ravenshead, Nottinghamshire NG15 8NA, United Kingdom, newsteadabbey.org.uk. Keats House, 10 Keats Grove, London NW3 2RR, United Kingdom, cityoflondon.gov.uk. Abbotsford, Melrose, Roxburghshire TD6 9BQ, United Kingdom, scottsabbotsford.com. The Abbotsford Trust, Abbotsford, Melrose Roxburghshire TD6 9BQ, United Kingdom, scottsabbotsford.com.
Pages 156–161: The Kilns, Headington, Oxford, OX3 8JD, United Kingdom, cslewis.org/ourprograms/thekilns. C. S. Lewis Foundation, 301 9th Street, Redlands, CA, cslewis.org.

RECIPE INDEX